MEET THE TEAM

PUBLISHER

Linda F. Radke, Linda@StoryMonsters.com

Author: Linda F. Radke

EDITOR-IN-CHIEF

Cristy Bertini, Cristy@StoryMonsters.com

WRITERS

Julianne Black DiBlasi, Raven Howell

SPECIAL CONTRIBUTORS

Judy Newman, Olivia Amiri, Deedee Cummings, Terrel Lefferts, Nick Spake

DESIGN & WEB MANAGEMENT

Jeff Yesh

PROOFREADER & CURRICULUM WRITER

Deb Greenberg

ADVERTISING

Cristy Bertini, Cristy@StoryMonsters.com

BOOK REVIEWERS

Christine Irvin, Dawn Menge, Cynthia Kern OBrien, Kimberly Waters, Mark Graham, Rachelle Stanger

PROMOTE YOUR BOOK IN OUR NEXT ISSUE!

Would you like to promote your book, product, or business? Contact Cristy Bertini at Cristy@StoryMonsters.com or call 413-687-0733 to reserve your space! Discounts available.

BRING *STORY MONSTERS INK* INTO YOUR CLASSROOM!

Visit our website at StoryMonstersInk.com to download free classroom question sheets to aid in learning comprehension and encourage your students to discuss what they've read in each issue!

SUBSCRIBE

Subscribe online or through digital subscription services for schools and libraries.

StoryMonstersInk.com

FOLLOW US

 Facebook.com/StoryMonsters

 @StoryMonsters

 instagram.com/storymonsters

 linkedin.com/in/storymonsters/

 youtube.com/@storymonsters

Studio Story Monster® is now open! Creating the music and graphics to help bring your story to life.
Click Here

HONOR ROLL

Named Among the "Great Magazines for Kids and Teens"
by *School Library Journal*

Mom's Choice Awards
Gold Award Recipient

2018 Irwin Award Winner
"Best Magazine Writer of the Year"

2016 Irwin Award Winner
"Best Publisher of a Literary Magazine" and "Best Editorial Director"

ISBN: 978-1-58985-338-6

Story Monsters Ink is published by Story Monsters LLC

Postal mail may be sent to
Story Monsters Ink
4696 W. Tyson St., Chandler, AZ 85226
Phone: 480-940-8182

AUGUST 2024

FEATURES

COLUMNS

RESOURCES

ONLINE

Check out StoryMonstersInk.com to keep up with book news, feature interviews, and more!

COMMENTS

Tell us what you think of this issue!
cristy@storymonsters.com
linda@storymonsters.com

Nandi Bushell

Drums Up Magic

by Raven Howell

Fourteen-year-old British musician and singer-songwriter Nandi Bushell is now adding "author" to her impressive résumé with the release of *The Life-Changing Magic of Drumming*.

Born in South Africa and now residing with her family in the United Kingdom, a young Nandi showed a strong interest in keeping a beat and drumming by the early age of five. Her parents nurtured her curiosity and enthusiasm. They bought her a drum kit. She began taking lessons.

"I would watch the 'Hey Jude' video on YouTube while making pancakes for breakfast with my family. Ringo looked so happy with the biggest smile on his face. I just remember thinking drumming looks like fun," says Nandi. "After doing well in a math club, my mum and dad took me to a toy shop, and I picked a toy drum kit. That's how it all started."

"Having lessons has really helped me progress and improve. It's always nice to have someone to support you when you get stuck."

THE LIFE-CHANGING MAGIC OF
DRUMMING
by Musician
Nandi Bushell
Illustrated by Andrea Stegmaier

In subsequent years, with her father's assistance, Nandi posted covers of various popular songs she played to social media outlets. She quickly gained popularity around the globe and earned respect and admiration from several well-known music stars. "Never in a million years did I think all the incredible things that have happened to me would have when I first started posting musical covers."

She's performed on the biggest stages in music such as London's Wembley Stadium, and jammed with such heavyweights as Dave Grohl (of Foo Fighters and Nirvana fame), Lenny Kravitz, and with members of Red Hot Chili Peppers, Rage Against the Machine, and Queen.

"There have been many special performances," she says. "Playing with Lenny at the O2 arena at the age of nine was really special, as it gave me a taste of what it would be like to be on stage. Playing outside Buckingham Palace was incredible, but playing my first gig with the Foo Fighters at the Forum in L.A. was really incredible."

"I think both live drumming and studio drumming are fun, but there is nothing like playing to an arena or stadium full of people. It's an unreal experience."

Nandi released the cover of Nirvana's song, "In Bloom," in 2019. She says, "I came home from a 'Rock School Club' I was going to after school. I had just learned 'In Bloom' and wanted to show my family. My dad thought it was amazing and filmed my performance. I don't know why I let out a scream, it just happened. I guess I was just in the moment. That scream kind of changed my life. I think people connected to my performance. The video went viral." It gained over 10 million views on Twitter within just a week.

In August 2020, in the midst of the COVID-19 pandemic, Nandi uploaded a cover of "Everlong" by Foo Fighters, and challenged her favorite drummer, Dave Grohl, to a drum-off. Grohl responded by drumming along with "Dead End Friends" by his supergroup Them Crooked Vultures to return the challenge to Bushell. After she posted a video drumming to the same song, Grohl conceded defeat, which resulted in friendship.

That online drum battle garnered lots of attention, receiving international coverage. "The battle was a very special moment in my life that I don't think could ever be as special if I tried again. But I like the idea of collaborating now more than battling."

Confiding that Dave Grohl is her hero, she says, "He is not just the nicest guy in rock—he is the nicest guy in the world."

In 2021, Nandi felt honored to be one of several drummers invited to perform a cover of "Come Together" for the Why Hunger project organized by none other than Ringo Starr. She reveals, "It was amazing being included in the project. I hope one day I will get to meet Ringo in person and jam with him."

Nandi has made many videos, has had numerous TV appearances, and was the youngest artist featured on the cover of *Modern Drummer* magazine. In February 2021, Cartoon Network named Nandi their first official musician-in-residence. Today she's a world-famous musician.

Her debut book, *The Life-Changing Magic of Drumming* is a beginner's guide to drumming. Encouragingly, she says, "You can learn a lot from online lessons and books. I hope to be an inspiration to pick up an instrument. I also want to show people that extraordinary things can happen to ordinary people. I am just a normal 14-year-old. I have been very lucky, but have also practiced a lot. You have to be prepared for when opportunities happen."

The book includes everything from simple drum beat exercises to more complicated drum rolls, backbeats, and fills. Step-by-step instructions make things easy to understand, and the author offers insider tips, life lessons she's learned thus far, and advice to motivate young musicians.

"I am really lucky to be a published author at 14. I think my story is pretty unique and hopefully inspiring. I worked really hard thinking about the best life advice and drumming lessons I could give."

Even if you've never picked up a drumstick in your life, Nandi says, "There's helpful information for those with no experience at all, and a range of beats for beginners to intermediate. I hope my book offers aspiring musicians motivation to try something they have never done before and shows them that anything is possible with practice."

The Life-Changing Magic of Drumming is illustrated by Andrea Stegmaier. "Andrea's artwork is amazing," says Nandi. "I absolutely love her illustrations." The engaging pictures are delightfully smile-inducing, and on some pages, markedly significant as visual directives.

Regarding her career, Nandi asserts, "I am pretty determined and don't like to give up when things get difficult. I like challenges and setting myself goals to work toward. As long as I have a goal I am working toward, I stay motivated. And I am working on new original songs all the time," she says. "I will start releasing more music in the future."

At home, she likes reading, relaxing, playing computer games, watching movies, and hanging out with her friends. Her family and dog, Marli, are dear to her, and she considers her life ordinary. "I go to school, I do homework, I hang out with my friends. People sometimes think I live a rock star life, but I am just a very lucky, ordinary 14-year-old."

"The real world is magical enough. It's possible to make your dreams come true with a lot of hard work and a bit of luck. Ask for what you want but make sure you are prepared for when your request is answered."

Playfully, Nandi adds, "And if drums had three rules, they would be practice, practice, practice plus have fun!"

For more information about Nandi and her work, follow her on Instagram @nandi_bushell.

Some lessons are difficult to learn...

Jenny's Journey is the story of a girl who has suffered tragic loss and difficult circumstances, making her vulnerable to making a regrettable choice that leads to an unintended and dramatic outcome. Includes key questions to help parents, teachers, counselors, and youth workers facilitate discussions on how to navigate through peer pressure, make good decisions, and use good coping skills.

Chapter Book for Ages 10+

"Nita Brady has done it again. Real and compelling—taking you on a journey that many of us have gone through, and our children go through today. I loved it. A must-read for parents and children alike. Nita has a remarkable gift at infusing life lessons in an attractive story filled with struggle, grief, loss, love, connection, addiction, peer pressure, triumph, and near-death experiences. Thank you, Nita, for saving our children."

—Michael Baldwin, CEO, Legacy Alliance Outreach

www.drugprevention4kids.com

Frank Payne

Embarks on a Tail-Wagging Adventure

by Raven Howell

During his childhood, Frank Payne would go fishing with his grandfather on the Rappahannock River in Falmouth, VA. Little did he know the influence it would have on his future creative efforts.

Frank's first picture book, *Webster the Beagle,* published in 2018 by Mascot Books, tackles the subject of fitting in and finding one's true home. Webster, born a hunting dog, gets lost in the woods until he's taken in by a loving owner. With the kindness and support of his new family, Webster's life changes. He's able to express his full potential and brings happiness to everyone around him.

Long familiar with dogs, Frank says, "We had two pups growing up: a cocker spaniel named Happy, and a basset hound named Sorry. I grew up at a time when our parents pretty much kicked us out of the house in the summer from sunup to sundown. We would go to our grandparents a lot, which was the best because that meant time on the river and fishing. Other times I'd be in my neighborhood, doing all the normal things—riding bikes, playing Kick the Can and every sport available—basketball, baseball, football, soccer, running."

"My siblings and I were all readers as kids. My mom was a teacher and volunteered at our local library by driving the bookmobile, and she made sure our summer reading list was always completed by June."

"I now live with my wife, Caren, and our two dogs, an Envigo rescue beagle named Billy (Envigo was the name of the company in VA where 4,000 beagles were rescued) and a black labrador, River, and our extended family and large group of friends. I'm an avid outdoorsman, tennis player, and fan of all things James Madison University. I am also active in my community and enjoy exploring new ventures—from owning racehorses to oyster farming," he says.

Accomplishing his ambitions of wanting to own a business or be a politician, Frank is the vice president of sales and a minority owner of PD Brooks, a traffic control company in Richmond, VA. "And every day, I look forward to making

someone's day better with an act of kindness or just a smile and hugging my dogs."

His choice for the beagle as the subject of his books was not haphazard. Frank says, "As an owner, once you have one, it's so hard not to have another and then another and another ... I love their curiosity, loyalty, fierceness, and although small, how big their personalities and hearts are. Beagles make great therapy dogs and are small so they can get into beds with the patients."

Furthermore, there is a deeper connection between the stories Frank wrote to real life. "I have always loved trying new things and meeting new people, and I have also made sure that everyone I meet feels welcome and hopefully feels that they have made a new friend. Webster is a true story about a special dog that makes everyone feel better."

His inspiration for *Webster the Beagle* was intact, yet Frank says he surprised everyone, including himself at writing and publishing his books. "My older brother is a lawyer who is always reading and writing, and my younger sister is in public relations, so I think everyone was stunned when I, running a

business, was the one writing children's books," he chuckles. "It was also very easy, and my publishing company helped me the whole way."

Due to the success of the first book, Frank was asked to write another one. "The feedback has been overwhelming in the best way," he says. "My favorite reaction is always with kids. When I do readings, kids always ask me if Webster really wore costumes—yes! I think the connection simply comes from not only what dogs mean to us but the sense of having a place to call home ... especially the special home in our hearts for our dogs."

For the new release, *Webster the Beagle and His Adventures at the River,* it was life by the riverside that motivated Frank. The story's message is one of hope and never giving up on your dreams. "I had been thinking about Webster and our love for the Rappahannock River. I thought how fun it would be to include our adventures there. It's a special place and the dogs really love it. All of the animals that live on the river or in the river inspired that story," he says.

The book includes a fun educational aspect with several pages containing fascinating facts about river life. "The

book is through the eyes of Webster, the beagle, and how he experiences the river, but I added an educational way to teach children and adults fun facts they might not have known. Most people don't know facts about animals they see and live with on a daily basis. I thought it was important to include a variety of animals that live on or in the river and tell some important 'Did you know' information about each of them and the seasons they thrive in."

Frank is happy to have collaborated with illustrator Romney Vasquez for both books and shares his favorite part of the story. "It's definitely when Webster gets pinched on the nose by a crab! And yes, this really happened! I tried to warn him but like all beagles, he thought he knew better and just had to stick his nose in where it didn't belong! Also, when he would venture next door to see the neighbors. They loved him so much that this was what eventually made him think of him becoming a therapy dog."

Appreciatively, Frank says, "Two of the biggest rewards I receive are, first, the looks on kids' faces when they're reading the book or I'm reading to them, and the second, when I get to donate to an organization that means so much to me because of Webster. All profits and proceeds of the books are gifted to non-profits. Their causes mean a lot to my family. The organizations are MCV Children's Hospital in Richmond, VA, local little league teams, local SPCA and senior dog rescues."

"A good tip if you're considering adopting a puppy is to make sure it's the right fit for you and your family. All dogs are cute,

but your lifestyle may not match theirs and vice versa, so it's really important to make sure you're a match but usually you know—it's like magic when that connection happens. The best thing about dogs is how they bring so much comfort and joy into our lives." Amused, Frank says, "Who would believe a dog inspired me to become a writer!"

His new book holds significance. "I wanted to share the wonderful world of river life, and the experiences one can have from time spent there, from fishing and crabbing to watching the birds. The Northern Neck and specifically the Rappahannock River in Virginia is a beautiful, special place." He concludes, "I hope people are inspired to enjoy any river with their loved ones."

For more information about Frank Payne and his work, visit websterthebeagle.com or follow him on Instagram @beaglewebster.

Dawn Renee Young

Inspires Kids to Make Good Choices

by Raven Howell

"I stay motivated because I love children and try to instill in them the love of literacy and the importance of making good choices for a lifetime," says children's author Dawn Renee Young.

Dawn is a retired teacher, principal, and teacher improvement coordinator, and obtained a degree as an Educational Specialist in Character Education. She's published the *Mrs. Good Choice* line of books and continues to present her program, "Good Choices Matter," in schools and libraries.

"I began my writing journey back in 2012. My debut book, *The ABCs of Making Good Choices*, was published in 2013 by a local college here in Tennessee. I self-published seven books in the *Mrs. Good Choice* series from 2013-2015. After that venture, I began writing almost every day for the next seven years. I have written over 50 picture book manuscripts. Then in 2023,

TAP - TAP - TAP
written by
Dawn Renee Young
illustrated by
Marla Taylor

I was picked up by Solander Press and also one of my books was published by a division of Harper Collins Christian."

She says, "I always wanted to write, but due to my busy career I didn't have time. After being a principal, I worked as a Teacher Improvement Coordinator which freed up some of my time. That's when I wrote my first manuscript. I have written 14 picture books and my own memoir, *My World of Light and Love...by Dawn*."

Dawn feels her biggest reward from publishing books is sharing them with children during author visits. "The excitement on those sweet faces and the great questions they ask at the end of each program are amazing."

"My author visits have definitely evolved over the years. When I first started, I had a Mrs. Good Choice Puppet made. I still use her with the younger children. I like to gear my visits to the needs of the school. All visits are very interactive through stories, songs, and dance. I read different books to different grade levels. With the older grades I share my writing process," she says.

"I think picture books are important because it is a child's first experience with written text. Also, they can learn about the world around them with the help of illustrations." Dawn had many of her own favorites from childhood, including *Little Women*, the *Nancy Drew* series, and *The Best Christmas Pageant Ever*.

She presently lives with her family in Tennessee, but grew up in a small town in Magnolia, Ohio. "I was raised by wonderful hard-working parents who instilled in me the value of perseverance and the love of books and reading. What most people don't know about me is that I was born with a vision impairment that is not correctable with glasses. My parents were told that I needed to go to a school for blind children. That never happened! I always say the two things I don't do is drive or play tennis. Ha! I did, however, take up golf three years ago," she says with jocularity.

Dawn considers perseverance the trait that has helped her most. She feels she's gathered several important lessons from her life experiences.

- Children can't help who their parents are.
- Never compare siblings.
- All children just want to be loved.
- Little eyes and little ears are always watching and listening.
- It's our job as adults to be great role models for today's children.

Dawn's new book, *Liam's Big Surprise,* won an Honorable Mention in the 2024 Purple Dragonfly Book Awards. The book tackles issues related to new family additions from a child's point of view. "The most wonderful thing about writing *Liam's*

Big Surprise is that my daughter-in-law was pregnant with our third grandchild," says Dawn. "I could imagine my six-year-old grandson and three-year-old granddaughter asking a lot of questions about the new arrival."

She released another book this year, titled *Loose at the Zoo*. In *Loose at the Zoo*, Sam and his beloved pet, Gus, are enjoying a day at the zoo until Gus gets loose, causing a bit of havoc. "*Loose at the Zoo* offers a new perspective to children. It shows them that sneaking behind their parents' backs may not always be a good choice. I feel that my lifetime of working with children has given me a great perspective on how children act and what they like. I try to convey that in my stories."

"My most challenging aspect of starting a new project is the long process of revisions. I do belong to a critique group that meets monthly to share manuscripts. It is important as a writer, to leave room for the illustrator and the reader to help figure things out," she contends.

"I love visiting my grandchildren and seeing the world through their eyes. It often gives me inspiration for a new topic to write about. I am very happy in my life right now. I am married to a wonderful man who often attends school visits with me. We have three amazing grandchildren, ages one, four, and seven who are the light of our lives. And ... I am beginning to fill up my fall calendar with school visits."

Dawn is especially enthusiastic about a new project. "I am excited to announce that my first early chapter book is just released. It's titled *Operation Laughter*. It has already received a Readers' Favorite Five Star Review."

"Laughter is medicine for the soul, a lesson young Millie learns from her grandfather." Explaining the premise, she says, "The story follows Millie as she tries her best to launch *Operation Laughter*. As she sets out to spread joy, she discovers that making people laugh is easier than learning when not to be a joke teller!"

Dawn muses, "I would love my books to travel to all 50 states and be available in all libraries for kids to check out. A bigger dream would be for some of them to be published in different languages."

"I think it is extraordinary when I meet a child out in public who has been to one of my school visits and they remember me." Cheerily, she adds, "I'm trying to change the world ... one child at a time."

For more information about Dawn Renee Young and her books, visit mrsgoodchoice.com. ●

Scott Sollers

Pens a Tall Tale for Little Readers

by Raven Howell

Children's author Scott Sollers tries to follow three guiding principles when appropriate. "Whatever you are doing, do the very, very best you can, because somebody is watching and it's not who you think it is. Second, take an interest in others. Ask questions and draw them out. You will learn something and forge a relationship that could be very meaningful. And lastly, always trust your instincts. You have a predisposition for a lot of reasons. Trust yourself," he encourages.

His new book, *A Tall Tale, How the Ostriches Got Their Long Necks and Long Legs* (Mascot Books), tells the story of rival communities, the Have-Alls and the No-Haves. The No-Haves, jealous of the Have-Alls' pets (called the Squatz) decide to try stealing them, causing a fierce tug-of-war between the two camps. When the air clears, the communities come together, choosing companionship and abundance and a fun surprise involving "how the ostriches got their long necks and long legs."

A Tall Tale is the new book in Scott Sollers' *Stephanie's Stories* series. "I think all of my stories try to show how selflessness and putting another's interest ahead of your own always produces positive results," says Scott, from his home in

San Mateo, California. "I was inspired to write these stories to enhance my relationship with my young daughter and I conceived and wrote these stories almost 30 years ago! I bought a blank hardback book and hand-wrote and illustrated 13 of these stories as an heirloom, and just recently undertook the daunting task of getting them published." He happily adds, "My publisher and marketing consultant have done superb work."

"I am very grateful to have had this and three other stories in publication and all should be released eventually. The publishing process takes time and work and I'm very pleased, and I want to wait a bit before I celebrate, but it will be a doozy!" he exclaims.

Scott grew up in Spokane, Washington, and he calls it an idyllic place to be raised. "Good climate and plenty of outdoor activities. My parents met during WWII and at one point during the war, my father was flying 37 missions over Germany as a bomber pilot for the RCAF, and my mother, born in Dundee, was driving an ambulance in London. We were raised by principled, caring parents."

Scott was an avid reader in childhood. "I read many books during the summer, including the *Horatio Hornblower* series, the *Caine Mutiny* trilogy, and many *Nancy Drew* mysteries. I loved these books, and they filled my imagination with rich scenes and character development."

"We moved around a bit in HS and at one of our stops, I learned to row crew in an eight-oared shell. I was recruited to go to the U of Penn for rowing, and I earned undergraduate and graduate degrees. My master's was in environmental sciences and since I had a low draft number during the Vietnam War, I did ROTC each summer. Because of that, the Army stationed me in Washington D.C. with the Corps of Engineers as an advisor to NASA. I did that for three years and met a number of brilliant people. After three years, I gave up my commission and moved to San Francisco where I ended up with a very satisfying career in municipal finance structuring bond issues for public agencies and I am still working as an advisor to my firm."

"My wife and I had two spectacular daughters and I shared different interests with each as they were growing up." Reminiscing, he says, "I would use Saturdays to take my older daughter on outings and I would spend bedtime with my younger daughter telling her these stories that I simply made up."

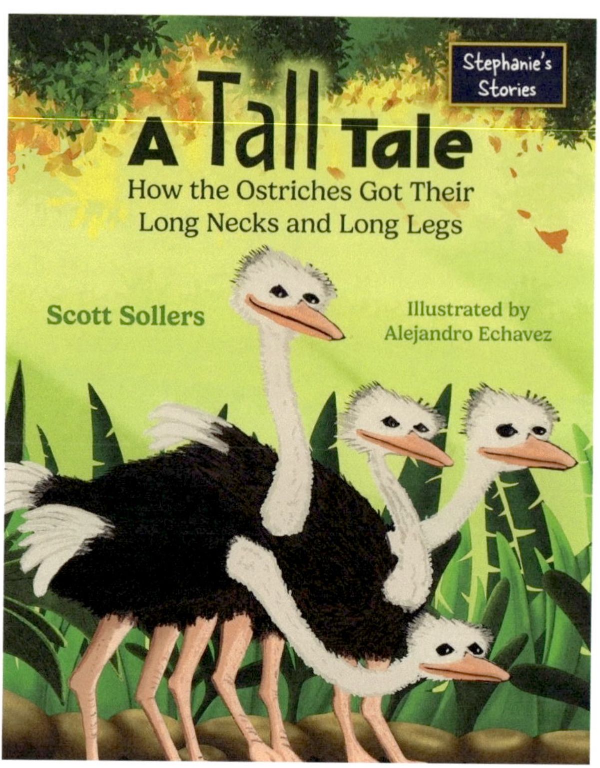

These days, he is an avid golfer, dotes on his lovable cat, Charlie, and says he tries to start each day with gratitude, humility, and some act of generosity. "I am generally on full throttle and have never had any problem being interested in our world and others and enjoying life!"

He describes himself as an "honest, hardworking, caring individual" and tries to find humor in everything. "All of my books are family-oriented, present a challenge or obstacle to overcome through understanding and teamwork, and there is always a satisfying outcome."

Scott's books have garnered the 2024 Purple Dragonfly Book Award, Mom's Choice Award Honoring Excellence, and the Literary Titan Award. Nevertheless, he finds that "the biggest reward is the caliber of the actual publication. The text and artwork are memorable. I am very gratified that it has resonated with critics, but what I love to hear is when a parent tells me their child wanted to have the book read several times in succession or the applause from kids when reading to a group."

He's continuing to write and has partnered with the San Francisco Zoo, which receives a portion the book's proceeds to benefit their African Savanna Habitat. They currently have two female ostriches, Daru and Bernadette.

"Presently, I have books with very different topics and scenarios in production. *Lake Omigosh* is about a lake in New Hampshire that has a creature who appears occasionally, and when seen, people exclaim, "Oh, My Gosh." Youngsters breaking camp rules go out into the lake and something happens to them and the creature. *The Dancing Shoes* is about a little girl who desperately wants to be a ballerina but lacks confidence and isn't very good. Her mother provides special confidence when she gives her ballerina shoes that belonged to her own mother. The story evolves with a surprise ending. And *How Flowers Got Their Colors* is about a shepherd who lives in a land where flowers and most everything are white and how he captures some colors from a rainbow, causing everything to change."

Scott offers advice to young authors. "Let your imagination run wild, pay attention to character development, and strive for a fulfilling and positive outcome."

For more information about Scott Sollers and his work, visit **scottsollersauthor.com** or follow him on Instagram @scottsollersauthor.

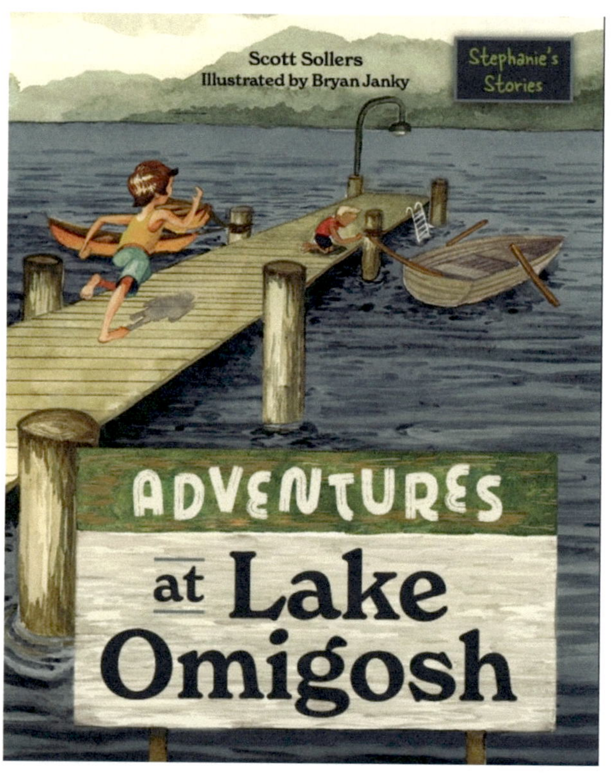

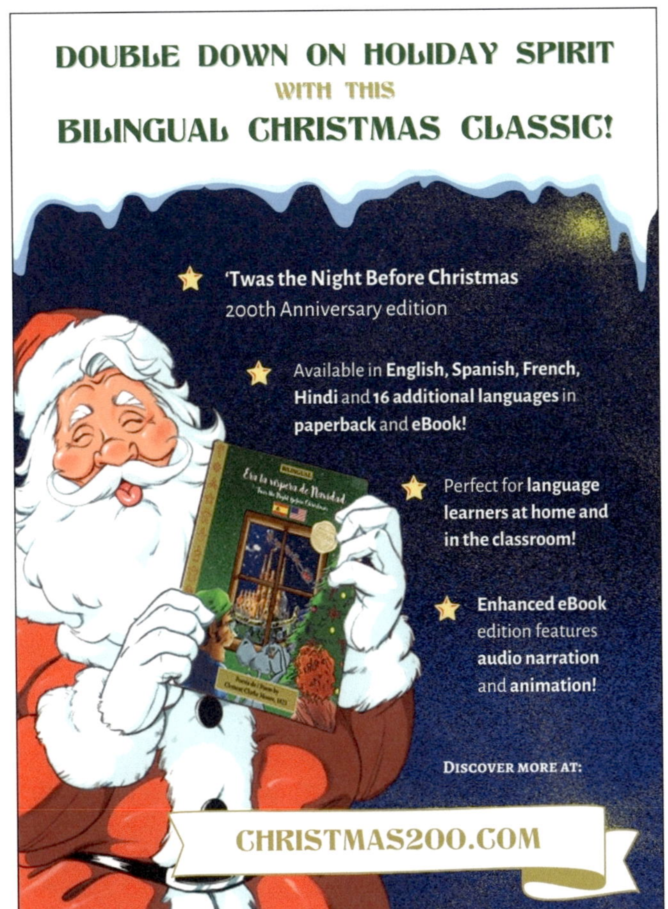

DOUBLE DOWN ON HOLIDAY SPIRIT
WITH THIS
BILINGUAL CHRISTMAS CLASSIC!
'Twas the Night Before Christmas
200th Anniversary edition
Available in English, Spanish, French, Hindi and 16 additional languages in paperback and eBook!
Perfect for language learners at home and in the classroom!
Enhanced eBook edition features audio narration and animation!
DISCOVER MORE AT:
CHRISTMAS200.COM

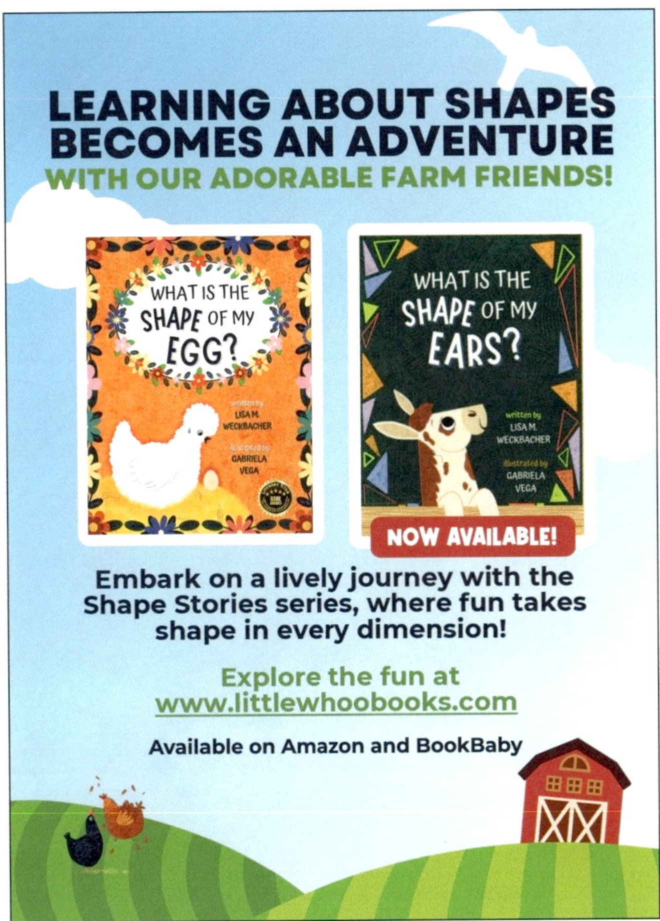

LEARNING ABOUT SHAPES BECOMES AN ADVENTURE
WITH OUR ADORABLE FARM FRIENDS!
WHAT IS THE SHAPE OF MY EGG?
WHAT IS THE SHAPE OF MY EARS?
written by LISA M. WECKBACHER
illustrated by GABRIELA VEGA
NOW AVAILABLE!
Embark on a lively journey with the Shape Stories series, where fun takes shape in every dimension!
Explore the fun at
www.littlewhoobooks.com
Available on Amazon and BookBaby

Help Children Build Resilience!
Encourage kids to find their inner strength with this fun and engaging picture book from bestselling authors Julia Cook and Michele Borba.
With the help of his friends, Charlie sets out on a big adventure to reach the top of the tallest mountain. Along the way, he learns six BOUNCE BACK SUPERPOWERS that allow him to think creatively, overcome challenges, and stay on the path.
I Got This!
I Have BOUNCE BACK Superpowers
Written by Julia Cook and Michele Borba, Ed.D
Illustrated by Dale Crawford
Available wherever books are sold.
NATIONAL CENTER for YOUTH ISSUES
www.ncyi.org

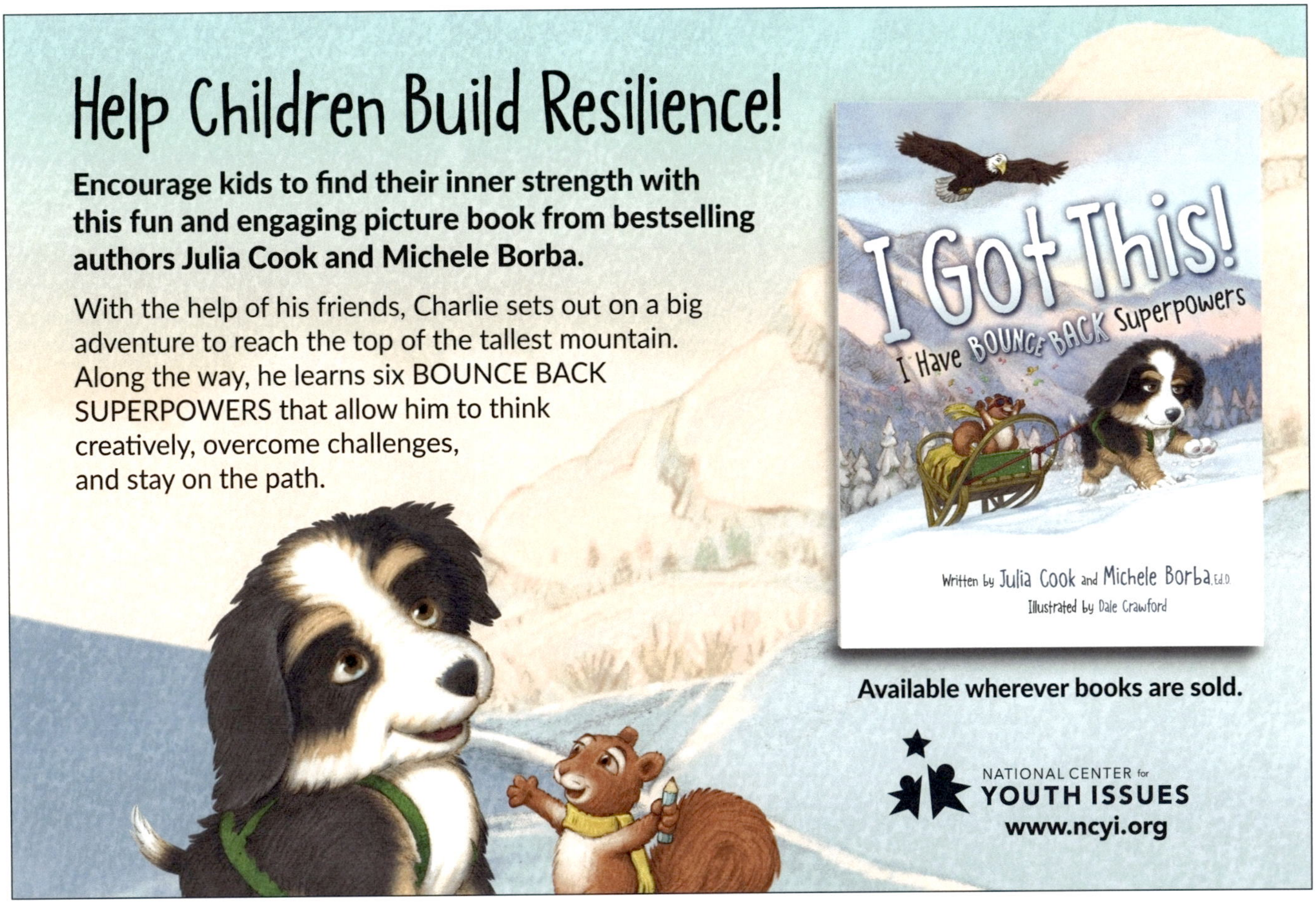

Aisha Saeed

Inspires Kids (and Grown-Ups) to Celebrate Everyday Joys

Meet Zuni. She's sweet, silly, ever-so-charming, and full of bright ideas. Her family has a memory jar. Anytime someone in the family does something important, they mark those moments through notes and photos stored in the jar and share those memories together at the end of the year. A deceptively simple story for young and old alike, *Zuni and the Memory Jar* is a reminder to celebrate everyday moments in life along with grand achievements. We love this idea and asked author Aisha Saeed to tell us more!

photo by Bindu Liang

Tell us about your career and where you worked before you became a writer. What inspired those career choices?

Before becoming a writer, I was a second-grade teacher and later, an attorney who represented children. I represented kids with disabilities and chronic illnesses to ensure they received equal access to education. As a writer for young people, I feel grateful that while my job has shifted, my focus remains the same: children. As an author, I still get to have school visits and interact with students, which is so incredibly meaningful for me.

What inspired you to become a writer?

I've loved to write since I could put a pencil to paper. Telling stories is how I make sense of the world. While I never could have dreamed as a child that I could be a storyteller for a living, I am incredibly grateful because the work truly feeds my soul.

Tell us about *Zuni and the Memory Jar*! What inspired the book?

I was inspired to tell a story about the beauty of the ordinary and the everyday. *Zuni and the Memory Jar* is a story about a family that decides to make a memory jar to collect memories of notable events in their lives throughout the year. The youngest in the family, Zuni, is often told lovingly that one day she'll have notable events to contribute as well, but Zuni knows something they don't know: that everyday moments are notable and beautiful and worthy of remembering as well.

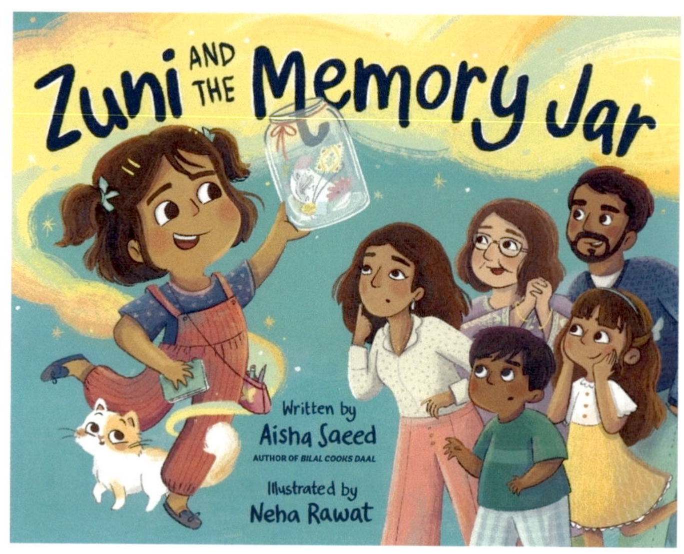

Do you keep your own memory jar?

Yes, we do have our own memory jar at home! We've had it for six years now. We collect all sorts of things in it from tickets from an event we attended, to programs for piano recitals, and other momentous occasions, but we also drop in memories that we handwrite on index cards of smaller moments, like when our cat did something incredibly silly, or someone told a joke that we couldn't stop laughing at. At the end of the year, we go through our memories and relive them and it's always so special.

When Mama comes home from her errands,
she pulls out a clear glass jar.

"For cookies?" Zuni asks.
"For memories!" Mama says.

Adam slips in a picture of his epic goal and then turns to Zuni.
"Don't worry, Zuni Zoo, someday
you'll have your own winning memories too."

At the final soccer game of spring,
GO JAGUARS!
Adam swerves, he dribbles, he scores.

The Jaguars win first place!
Thanks!

You are a founding member of the We Need Diverse Books Campaign. Has that work affected your storytelling?

I am so proud of all the work that WNDB does. This organization came about because of the lack of authentic diverse representation in the publishing landscape, particularly at the time. My storytelling, however, was always going to feature people who looked like my children, because growing up I never experienced authentic representation and I wanted to provide this. I am grateful to WNDB for raising more awareness to the importance of this. I truly believe they are the reason so many more writers from marginalized communities are able to write in the children's literature space today.

What is the best time of day for you to write? Are you a day writer or a night writer?

I write when my children are in school. At night I like to read. Reading is just as important as writing for me when it comes to growing and honing my craft.

What are some of your interests/hobbies outside of writing?

When I'm not writing, I'm baking with my children and doodling henna patterns.

What is your favorite writing snack?

My favorite writing snack would have to be a drink—chai. Which I am sipping right now, in fact. I love to have a bit of caffeine to start my mornings!

What are the most challenging aspects of your writing when you start a project?

I find the middle of stories to be the most challenging for me creatively. It's so fun to kick off a tale, and fun to reach the denouement, but the middle is just as important but takes a bit more work, so I often find myself spending the most amount of time there.

What advice would you give a first-time author?

I always tell aspiring authors to read as widely as they possibly can. I did not go to school to be a writer. I learned through loving books and stories and really studying the ones that resonated. I read about 50 books a year, and I feel like the more one reads, the better one grasps story fundamentals such as pacing and character development.

What's next for you?

Next up is actually a bit of a children's literature departure for me! I have an adult mystery coming out on February 4, 2025, *The Matchmaker*, about a matchmaker and suspenseful hijinks that ensue. While I'm excited for this adult novel, my heart is always going to be with children's literature and I have fun projects I'm working on in that arena as we speak that I hope to share more about soon!

What book are you reading now (aside from your own)?

I am currently reading *And Then, Boom!* by Lisa Fipps. It's a middle grade novel in verse about the challenges many kids face with housing insecurity and poverty. It's a powerful and engrossing read so far!

For more information about Aisha Saeed and her work, visit aishasaeed.com.

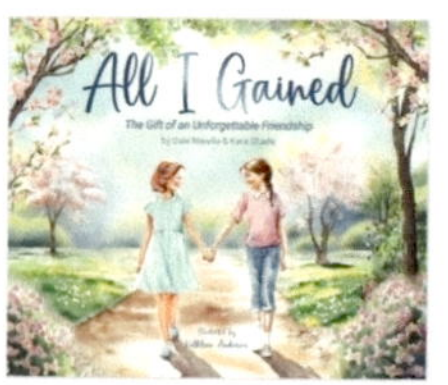

All I Gained: The Gift of an Unforgettable Friendship

by Dale Maiella & Kara Shade, illustrated by Kathleen Andrews

Two friends. Countless adventures. One incredible gift. A sweet bond between two unlikely grade school friends grows into an epic friendship spanning decades. Through their adventures and laughter, courage and heartbreak, Riley and Emma show us what it looks like to walk the path of life together faithfully, no matter what lies ahead. Written in rhyming verse with breathtaking watercolor illustrations, *All I Gained* offers a fresh take on friendship for older children and adults alike.

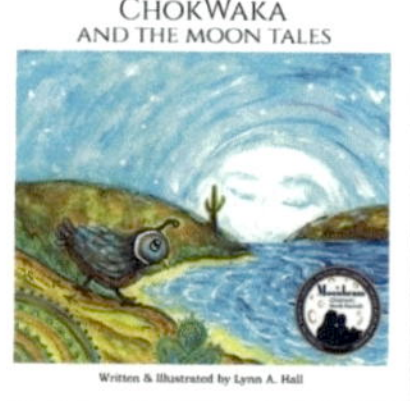

ChokWaka And The Moon Tales

by Lynn A Hall

A sweet children's environmental book about caring for each other and the Earth. Follow little ChokWaka as he happily learns from the lovely moon how we are all connected. Learn about Nature's ecosystems and how recycling plastics helps protect our oceans, food chains, and planet home. Enjoy sharing this beautifully illustrated and happy story teaching children we all belong and that every little voice matters! For ages 4-8.

Gertrude Garter Snake

by Paul Hock

My name is Gertrude Garter Snake. There are more of us than any other snake in North America. I was born fully formed but very tiny. Now I am fully grown, and can be a great help in your garden eating insects and other small critters that hurt your plants. Your plants are safe from me because I am a carnivore. I will never harm you either. To read more about me, go to **critteraweek.com**

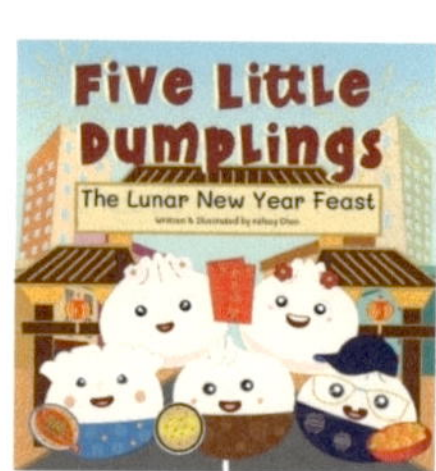

Five Little Dumplings: The Lunar New Year Feast

by Kelsey Chen

Join five little dumplings as they head over to Grandma's for Lunar New Year. Engage in a fun counting game and indulge in a cultural exploration. On their way to Grandma's for the New Year's Feast, the little dumplings engage in a fun counting game. From lanterns to sticky cakes, they count and have lots of fun. But that's just the start! The true excitement unfolds at Grandma's, with the festive dishes and decorations for the Lunar New Year.

Donkey Dell

by Jaybie D.

Donkey Dell's expressive snorts and unyielding glares showcase a personality unafraid to embrace his unique preferences. He often refuses to do anything he doesn't want to—"NO WAY!" After getting lost and gaining a new perspective, Dell sets off on an adventure that leads him to join the circus. Balancing on tightropes, mastering hula hoops, and more—until DISASTER STRIKES! Join Dell as he channels his determined strengths in an unexpected and inspiring way.

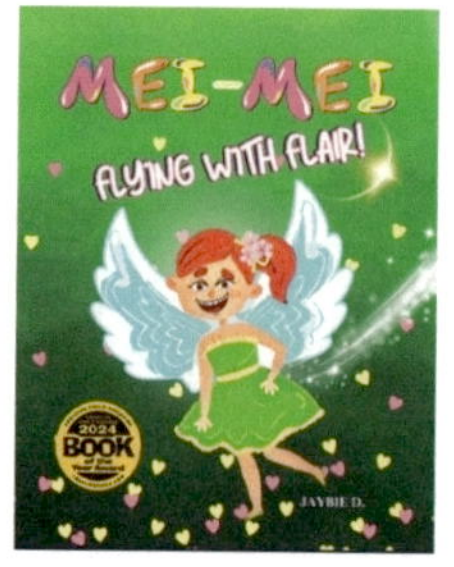

Mei-Mei Flying With Flair!

by Jaybie D.

Meet Mei-Mei (pronounced May-May), a curious fairy who discovers the power of resilience and self-reflection after an unexpected collision with a flock of birds. This story emphasizes the importance of mindful exploration and understanding before imitating others. Through Mei-Mei's journey of discovering what is in her heart, young readers are encouraged to celebrate their individuality, make informed decisions, and embrace the beauty of diverse perspectives that enrich our lives.

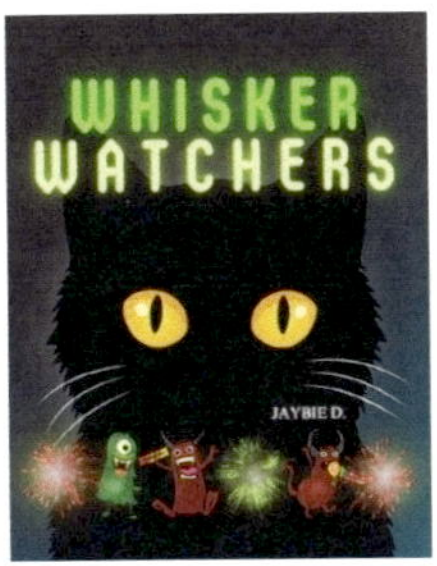

Whisker Watchers

by Jaybie D.

Whisker Watchers is a secret society of feline purr-tectors who prowl the night on Halloween. Their mission is to chase away candy-loving monsters and keep the kids safe. This book is a gentle introduction to the excitement of Halloween with a little bit of a thrill, so children know what to expect on the big night. Children will giggle with cheer, knowing that these purr-tectors are always near!

Sora Searches for a Song

by Once Upon a Dance

As the symphony floated above, Sora searched deep inside for a song. But nothing came. Melodies tickled across Sora's toes, legs, and back as the little cricket searched in vain for a song. Then a stern voice pierced the night, and the music stopped. "Someone's not singing." Readers are invited to stretch, balance, jump, and move along with all the creatures in this delightful story of perseverance and celebrating your own unique voice.

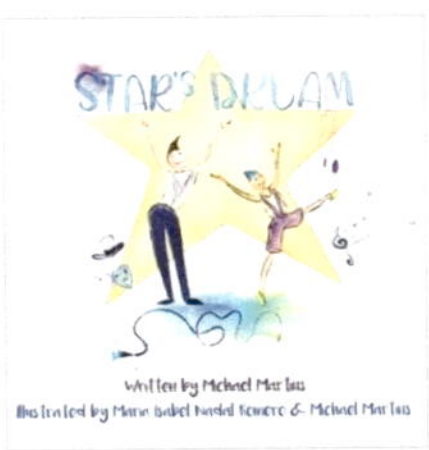

Star's Dream

by Michael Martins

Star's Dream is an introspective/self-reflective account inspired by the author's lived experiences. It focuses on character development, anti-bullying, and brave conversations written in simple language, and it makes sense of childhood challenges with attention to brave conversations using students' experiences in the early years program. This story is a call to acceptance/self-love and to dream big, in one very equitable read.

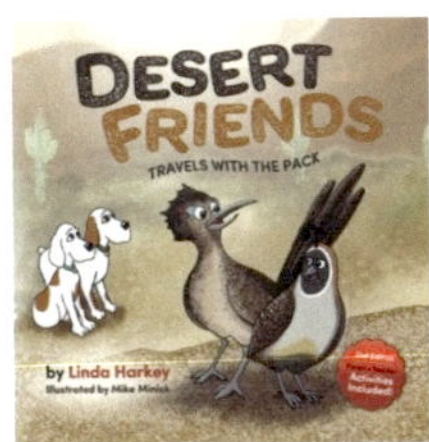

Desert Friends

by Linda Harkey

Animal friends in the Arizona Sonoran Desert are found in all sizes, shapes, and colors. Rodney, a Roadrunner and his best friend Quincy, a Gambel's quail spend days racing each other through dry creek beds called arroyos. One day Rodney and Quincy meet two hunting dogs—Gator and his three-legged buddy Tripod. Danger surrounds the four friends as a thunderstorm sends tremendous amounts of muddy water down the arroyo. The force of water sweeps Tripod away. Who will come to his rescue? What will happen when the Great One (the dogs' human hunter) arrives? harkeybooks.com

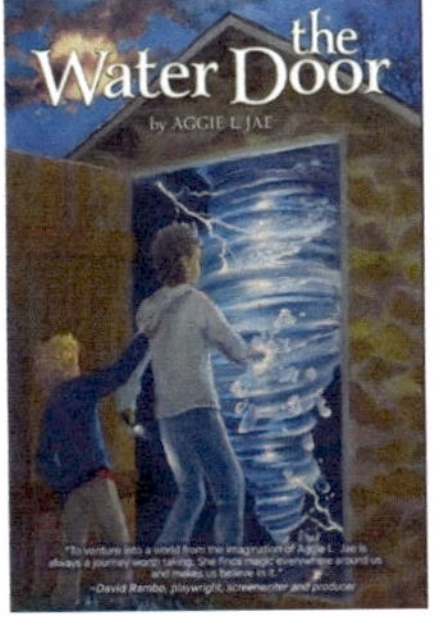

The Water Door

by Aggie L. Jae

Jeremy and Joshua are staying at their grandparents' farm when they discover The Water Door: a hydro-portal that transports them to the distant planet, Tetherae. Once there, the brothers embark on an exciting adventure through the Wilds of Tetherae that includes a fabulous treehouse, fierce dinosaurs, enormous giants, underground caverns, and mystical castles. Using their new Tetherae abilities, they must find a legendary heirloom diamond to rescue their parents from their evil uncle who has kidnapped them before time runs out.

I Am a Butterfly: A Story About Big, Beautiful Changes

by Sally Stone Ed.D.

This lovely children's book captures the science and splendor of the monarch's miraculous adventure from egg to butterfly. The author's own dazzling color photos guide the reader on the fascinating journey of metamorphosis and serve as a metaphor for the beauty to be found on the other side of surprising life changes. —Tierra Curry, Senior Scientist, Center for Biological Diversity. 1st Place, Purple Dragonfly Book Awards

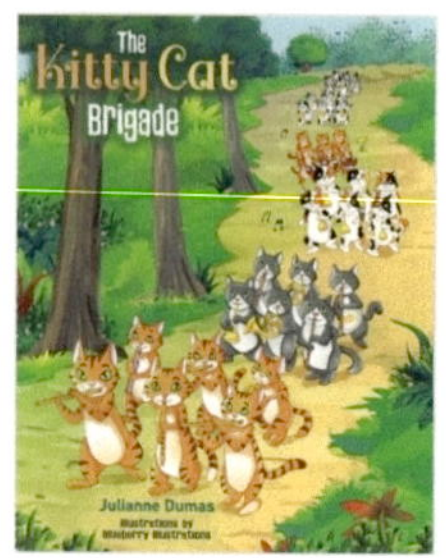

The Kitty Cat Brigade

by Julianne Dumas

Does your child have an imagination? Does your child love music? Do they love animals? Then they may enjoy reading *The Kitty Cat Brigade*. It is a picture book for children three to seven years of age and is wonderfully illustrated. This award-winning book features a band of cats who love playing music to the delight of their woodland friends. Join in the fun as the cats play their instruments and march along.

Wilda Reads at Recess

by Karen Georgiev

A whimsical story featuring a child who loves reading! The story reinforces emerging reading skills of alliteration and repetition in a relatable setting. It's sure to be a favorite!

Lou Can Too

by Mia McGlynn

Jump into construction and camaraderie with *Lou Can Too*, the sequel to *Bigger Diggers!* Lou, the mini excavator, arrives at a new job, joins a new team, and faces new challenges. This book is a bucket load of lessons about collaboration, acceptance, and the possibilities that come from supporting one another. Journey to a place where every machine, no matter the size, gender, or power source, has a special role to play!

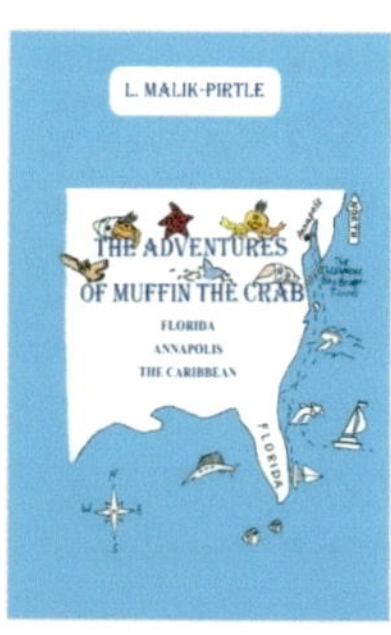

The Adventures of Muffin the Crab

by Leyla Malikova-Pirtle

This tale is about a crab, Muffin, who traveled with his human friend, Jeffrey, on an old sailing boat to Annapolis and then accidentally boarded the wrong yacht. Muffin is in for a big adventure with a grumpy barracuda, a nasty owl, raccoons, storms, and a whale with teeth problems. Afterward, he meets his new best friend Leonora. This heartwarming story shows that a hero is inside all of us, no matter how little we are.

The GIFTS Friends Give Us

by Deborah Burke Henderson

The GIFTS Friends Give Us, a middle grade chapter book, encourages self-discovery, the joys of family and friendship, and the core values of kindness, honesty, and respect. More than a sweet adventure story about loveable animal characters, *GIFTS* inspires children to believe in themselves while learning to appreciate the differences in others. Perfect for family read-alouds or classroom discussions. Fun Facts, a discussion guide, and a creative activity list follow this heartwarming story.

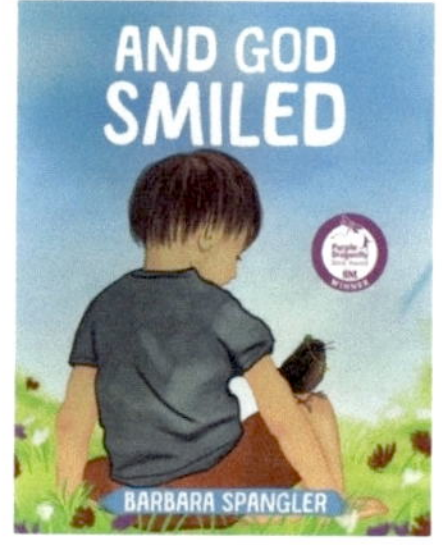

And God Smiled

by Barbara Spangler

This heartwarming tale imparts valuable lessons on environmental stewardship in a land where trees had long vanished. A little boy dreams of a lush forest on the barren lands. His wish leads him to a magical encounter with Little Sweet Pea Butter Bean, a charming house wren, who wears a garden pea for a hat, and the wise Red-Beet Bumble Bee. Together they embark on an extraordinary journey to bring back the forest.

Zippy Travels to Northeast

by Katie McManus

A tough-though-tiny hummingbird's captivating and inspirational story that illustrates the tenacity of a small creature and the profound impact it can have on the lives of those it touches. *Zippy Travels to Northeast* is not just a tale of survival in freezing Massachusetts; it is a story of friendship, resilience, and the extraordinary bond between humans and nature. The book underscores themes of adventure, the importance of family, and the power of perseverance.

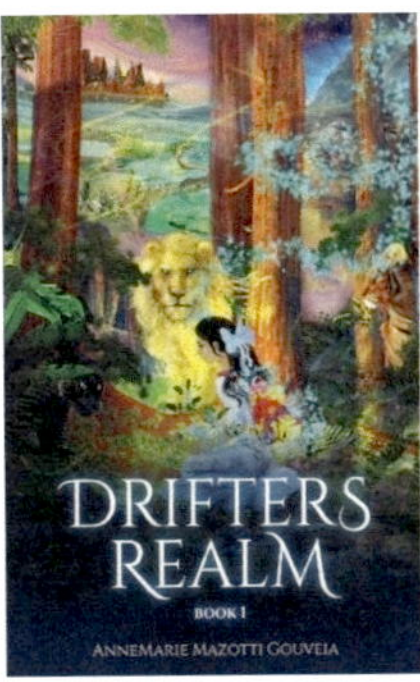

Drifters Realm

by AnneMarie Mazotti Gouveia

Twelve-year-old twins Ori and Roe, along with their older brother Theo, set out on a perilous journey in search of the truth about their father and the threat posed by the Menace to their way of life. As they journey, they must decide whether to fight against each other using their powers or to join forces to stop Quinlan and his daughter, Tora, who seek to destroy their peaceful existence. With the help of their unique backpack magic, transforming into a lion, or following a glowing ring to a magical blue pool under the stars is possible in this compelling story of survival and the power of friendship and family.

Mirror Tree

by AnneMarie Mazotti Gouveia

In book two of the award-winning *Drifters Realm* fantasy adventure series, Life Giver Roe, Sorcerer Ori, Tamer Theo, and Storm Catcher Tora, four estranged siblings with magical backpacks, race against time to solve an age-old prophecy foretelling an uprising and war. Along their daring journey, they discover a locked box, meet the Ghost of Ruin, and unearth family secrets that hold clues to finding the elusive Shadow Stone and Mirror Tree—critical elements in saving their mystical world, Drifters Realm. Kirkus Reviews praises the characters and the story, "A robust, magical cast propels this diverting fantasy."

Visitant: The Hidden Genome

by Pamela Cannalte

Humans have been on a path of self-destruction for ages but have been guided by forces and beings from alternate universes since the beginning of time, helping mankind through genetic manipulation. As the human species careen toward self-extinction, alien DNA surfaces in select doctors, scientists and gifted intellects around the world. We follow a specially gifted group of superhumans, including adolescent Grace, who possesses super-human abilities, on a preordained path to save the world. 2022 Purple Dragonfly Book Awards Winner in the Science Fiction and Young Adult Fiction categories!

Mr. Washington's Granite State Vacation

by Angela Welch

In the fall of 1789, George Washington decided to visit the northern states to talk about the new Constitution. He wanted to meet and listen to the people he met along the way. During his trip, he crossed the Merrimack River in Massachusetts, heading for Portsmouth, New Hampshire, the capital of the state at that time. Come along as President Washington takes his Granite State vacation.

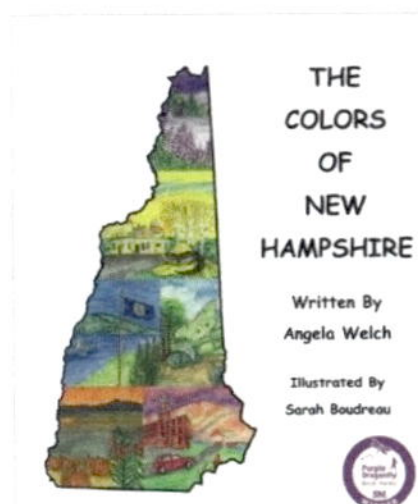

The Colors of New Hampshire

by Angela Welch

If you've ever visited New Hampshire in the fall, you've seen all the beautiful vibrant colors everywhere you turn. It looks like nature painted the landscape with deep reds, yellows, oranges, and browns. Yet, all through the year, New Hampshire displays crisp vivid colors whether it be ordinary objects or spectacular landscapes. Read about our state and its colors. Maybe it's time to plan a visit.

Blame It On Revere!: The Portsmouth Alarm

by Angela Welch

Paul Revere's famous ride in April of 1775 is well known by many. However, his first ride took place on a cold, stormy day in December of 1774 where he headed to the quiet coastal town of Portsmouth in the colony of New Hampshire. What message was so important that led to this journey? Read about the ride that led to the first shots of the American Revolution before those at Concord and Lexington, Massachusetts. www.lunabooksnh.com

The Imaginary

Grade: B

reviewed by Nick Spake

In the past year, there have been two movies about imaginary friends. Where John Krasinski's *IF* followed a Pixar blueprint, *The Imaginary* draws on the same lines as Studio Ghibli. This makes sense, as Studio Ponoc was founded by former Ghibli producer Yoshiaki Nishimura. Several Ghibli employees followed him to Studio Ponoc, which kicked off with the stunning *Mary and the Witch's Flower*. *The Imaginary* is another dazzling film that comes close to replicating Ghibli's magic. That said, Studio Ponoc is still living in Ghibli's shadow. Even the studio's logo is trying to mimic Ghibli, but Ponoc has yet to find its Totoro.

Most stories like this center on a child with an active imagination. In a refreshing spin, this adaptation of Emily Gravett's book is told from the perspective of an imaginary friend. Rudger came to Amanda shortly after her father died. As her mother tries to keep a roof over their heads, Amanda and Rudger go on adventures without leaving the house. When Amanda is involved in an accident, Rudger's fate is also left hanging in the balance. Without Amanda to remember him, Rudger risks fading away. Rudger seeks sanctuary in a land outside reality where Imaginaries can live forever. Without Amanda, though, Rudger struggles to find purpose.

The Imaginary is a spellbinding animation showcase. Akin to the bathhouse in *Spirited Away*, every imaginary friend here has an arresting design, leaving the audience to wonder what their backstory is. It's no surprise that director Yoshiyuki Momose was a key animator on *Spirited Award*. He also served as a director of animation for the game *Ni no Kuni*, which made the player feel as if they were living in an anime world. Every set piece in *The Imaginary* is like a rollercoaster, although the ride can change in the blink of an eye. You never know what wild visuals the filmmakers will throw our way next.

The film does a respectable job at establishing its rules with consequences that stick. As creative as this world is, *The Imaginary* can occasionally get bogged down by exposition. This is where Studio Ponoc could learn from Ghibli. Hayao Miyazaki typically doesn't dwell on the logistics of his films. He just plops us into worlds where witches casually co-exist with humans and a cat can be shaped like a bus. *The Imaginary* drags whenever it stops to explain its lore. The film's physical threats also aren't as compelling as Rudger's existential crisis.

The story shoehorns in a villain named Mr. Bunting, who feeds upon imaginary friends. While the concept is creepy, it's hard to take Mr. Bunting seriously with his Hawaiian shirt and a mustache like the Pringles guy's. Sometimes his facial expressions come off as unnerving. With Jeremy Swift providing his voice, though, all we're going to think of is Higgins from *Ted Lasso*. Not to dwell on Miyazaki, but his films rarely rely on one-dimensional villains to provide the conflict. This film didn't need to either.

The real heart of *The Imaginary* lies in the relationship between Rudger and Amanda. Rudger provides the escape Amanda needs as she copes with her grief. There will come a time, however, when these best friends have to part ways. These themes could've been elaborated on, especially in the third act. *The Imaginary* is nonetheless a thoughtful, surprisingly mature film that isn't afraid to explore loss. The downbeat moments are balanced with lively animation and a sincere relationship at the story's core. Ponoc has yet to reach the heights of Ghibli, but this feels like a solid stepping stone toward better things to come. Just keep mining that imagination. ●

Nick Spake is a member of the Hollywood Critics Association and Phoenix Film Critics Society. Follow him on Twitter at @NSpake and everywhere else at Nick Spake.

JUDY NEWMAN LIFE OF A READER

WE SCREAM FOR ICE CREAM ... AND READING!

by Judy Newman

My favorite ice cream flavor—hands down—is vanilla chocolate chip. I do like other options in the chip family: raspberry chocolate chip, mint chocolate chip, and peppermint chip. But since my childhood days of Friendly's, Brigham's, and Steve's Ice Cream in Somerville, MA—before all the fancy small batch flavors came to market—vanilla chocolate chip has always been my flavor of choice.

This week, Sophie Rae, almost four, already an ice cream aficionado, prefers strawberry. She likes a few baby marshmallows and a few chocolate chips buried in the middle of her cone. She also likes to have a second scoop. Two weeks ago, fudge swirl was her chosen flavor to sit on top of her strawberry base. The week before it was raspberry sorbet. By the end of the summer, she will have chosen a few more second-place flavors and it's even possible strawberry will get knocked off the #1 favorite spot.

Deciding which ice cream to put in your cone is serious business. We take all the ice cream cartons out of the freezer—even the ones with only a few shards of ice cream left in them that no one wants to throw out—and conduct an official taste test to determine what makes it into the cone.

Flavor by flavor, we each take a small spoonful and then Sophie marks our reactions—or X—in each box on the chart.

ICE CREAM	STRAWBERRY	FUDGE RIPPLE	Rasb. Sorbet	Mint Chocolate Chip
SOPHIE	+	+	+	+
JUYA	+		+	+
PA	+			+

Once we've cataloged our preferences, we put together double (or sometimes triple) scoop cones. We channel Steve Herrell and the "Smoosh-In™" he invented when he opened Steve's Ice Cream in Somerville, MA in 1973. We insert our own add-ins: baby marshmallows, chocolate chips, and jelly beans in between the scoops. Delicious and fun!

Sophie's continuously evolving preference for ice cream mirrors her continuously evolving preference—and hunger—

for the books she wants us to read with her. My goal for Sophie Rae—and for all children—is to make reading aloud and reading together (and eventually reading independently) as fun and delicious and reflective and respectful of her personal preferences as her adventures in ice cream. If she doesn't like the taste of what she's reading, she's not going to want to read that book, and if a book she doesn't like or isn't comfortable reading is forced on her, she may get turned off from reading altogether.

At the beginning of the summer, Sophie chose *Hot Dog* by Doug Salati to read every day. *Goodnight Hairiette* by Tanya Wright has been a favorite all summer and Sophie can recite whole passages of the story of Hairiette's grandmother growing up in Graytown from memory.

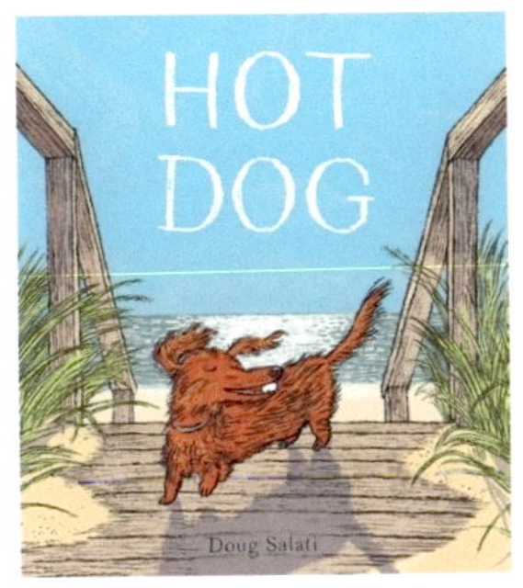

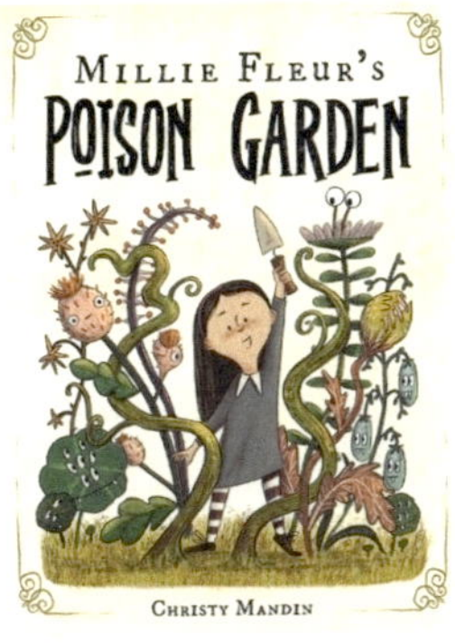

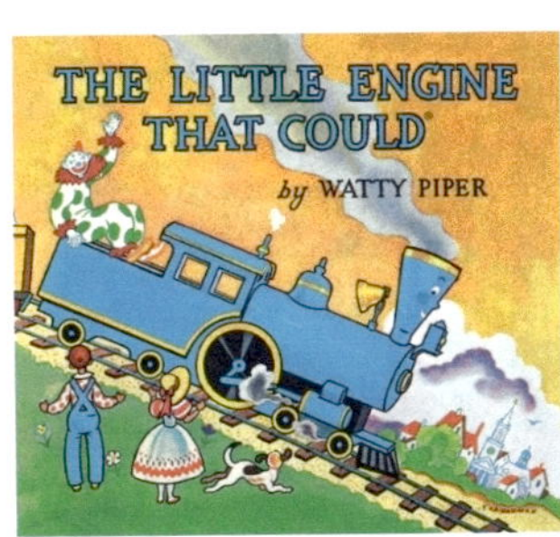

At the beginning of the summer, she wasn't so interested in *Millie Fleur's Poison Garden* but now she loves it and requests it again and again. *Millie Fleur* joins *The Little Engine That Could*—a very different book—as one of Sophie's favorites.

It's hard to get kids interested in reading when there is so much else going on around them. My message this summer—and all year round—is: Use every opportunity to insert a book into your day. And go with your child's preferences. Follow their lead on which books they are interested in and want to read. Don't insist they read one book or another. Let them choose!

There are also lots of great books about ice cream which are fun to read when you're eating a delicious cone with two scoops and hidden add-ins. But any book about any topic can make a great summer read. Here are some I've found:

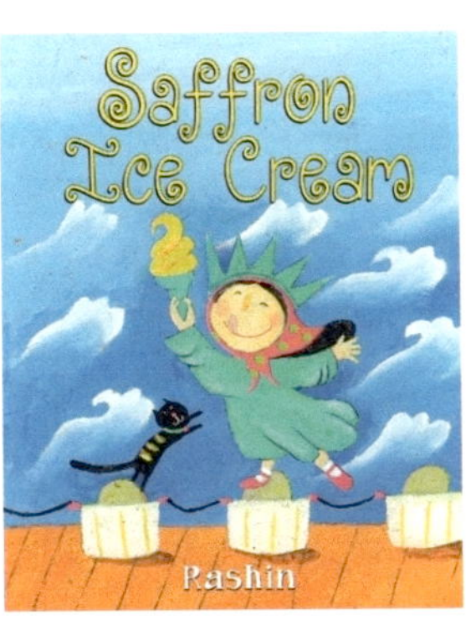

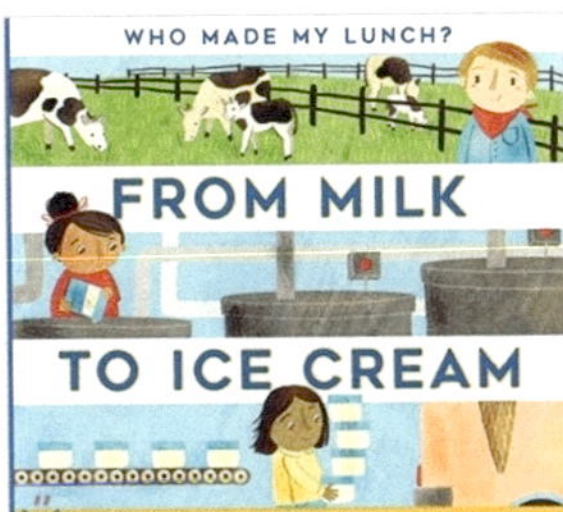

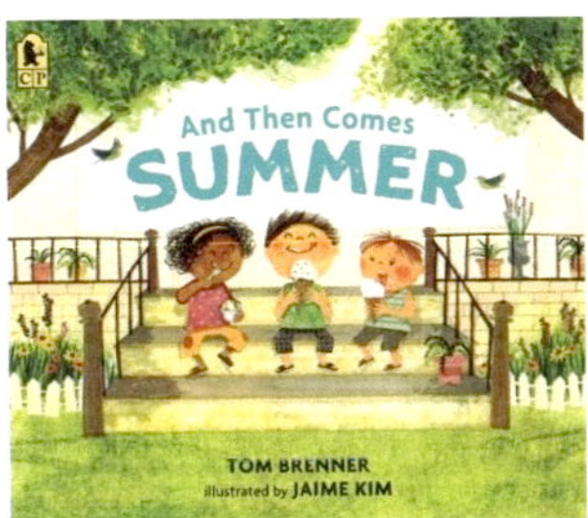

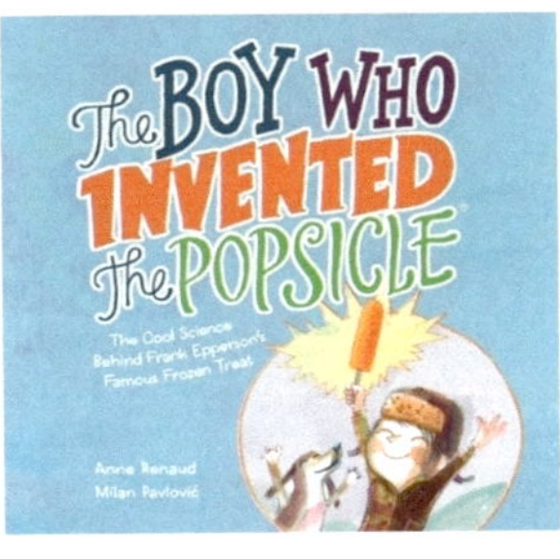

The key to helping every child develop their self-confidence as a reader is to follow their lead. Let them choose which books they want to read. And if they want to eat their cones while reading—even if some of that strawberry/fudge swirl combo with marshmallows tucked inside drips on the pages—that's OK! It all contributes to making reading a fun and happy time together, building a solid foundation for your child to declare: "I am a reader."

Judy

Judy Newman, Chief Impact Officer, Scholastic.

BOOK REVIEWS

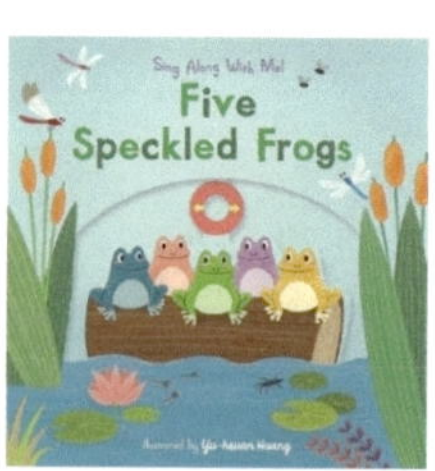

Sing Along With Me! Five Speckled Frogs

by Yu-hsuan Huang (Candlewick)

Reviewer: Lindsay Moretti

A fun and engaging take on the "Five Speckled Frogs" song, this board book includes chunky push-and-pull sliders, and a spinning wheel that animates the frogs throughout. Bright colors and friendly pond creatures are illustrated as the story transitions from day to night. Scan the QR code on the back to hear the song and sing along! (Baby-2)

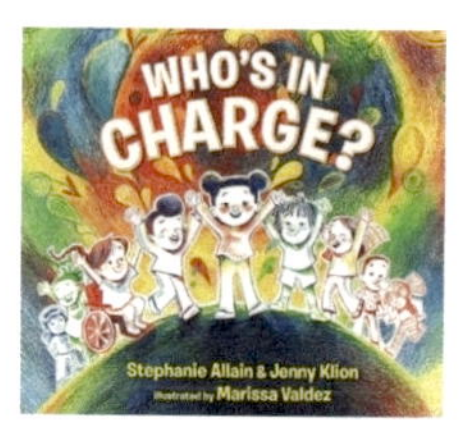

Who's in Charge?

by Stephanie Allain, Jenny Klion (Candlewick)

Reviewer: Rachelle Stanger

Who is in charge of your body? Your mind? Your feelings? You are of course! *Who's in Charge?* teaches young children about being responsible for their actions and everything they do. No one else gets to decide that, so the goal is to make good choices and take care of your own body and life! (Ages 2-5)

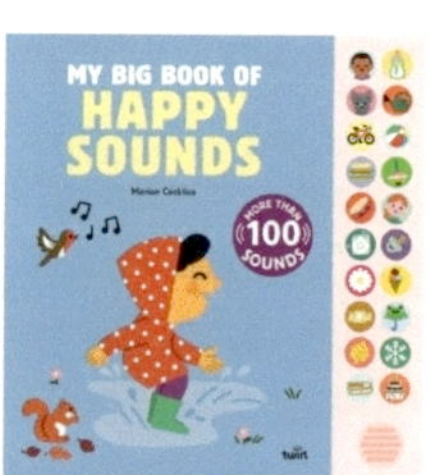

My Big Book of Happy Sounds

by Marion Cocklico (Twirl)

Reviewer: Lindsay Moretti

A delightful board book with diverse, colorful illustrations and sound panel. The 20-button panel corresponds to pages that represent sounds heard any time of day or season, or from various activities and occasions. With over 100 sounds, this book would be a great source of entertainment for little ones who are eager to explore and identify the sounds of their world. (Baby-3)

Winston

by Alysen Bayles (Austin Macauley)

Reviewer: Deb Greenberg

Winston is a unique dog ... he befriends bunnies instead of chases them, and he only wants to hang out with Sally (who took him in) and his best friend Bossy Bunny. Tiny tots will adore wonderful Winston in this lovable tale that's loosely based on an abandoned and abused dog rescued by author Bayles that became part of her family. (Ages 3-5)

It's Time to Hush and Say Good Night

by Chitra Soundar, Sandhya Prabhat (Candlewick)

Reviewer: Christine Irvin

This bedtime book was inspired by ancient Indian lullabies used to lull babies to sleep. Gentle rhymes, repetition, and expressive, swirling illustrations all work together to create a soothing end to the day when it's time to hush and say good night. (Ages 2-5)

The Elephant and the Sea

by Ed Vere (Doubleday Books)

Reviewer: Christine Irvin

Gabriel is an elephant whose dream in life is to join the crew on the lifeboat in his seaside town. At first, he is too little, so while waiting to grow big enough, he works on his rowing technique. When he's all grown up, he's then told he's too big to be on the boat. (He is, after all, an elephant.) Then, Gabriel has an idea, but will it work? A cute story (and one with a good message) and adorable illustrations make this a fun book for kids. (Ages 3-7)

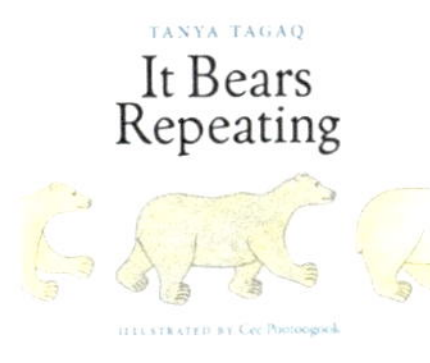

It Bears Repeating

by Tanya Tagaq, Cee Pootoogook (Tundra Books)

Reviewer: Cynthia Kern OBrien

Beginning with one proud polar bear standing tall and ending with 10 bears waving goodbye, this delightful counting book shows polar bears in all their forms: slippery and fast, crafty and cool, hungry and proud. Fun for kids to count along while they learn about polar bears and all of their daily activities. (Ages 3-7)

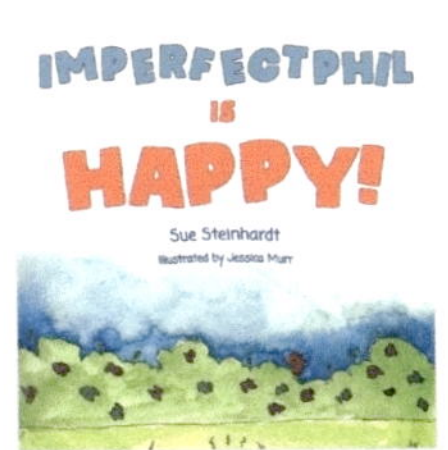

ImperfectPhil is Happy

by Sue Steinhardt, Jessica Murr (BC Books LLC)

Reviewer: Deb Greenberg

Book four in the *ImperfectPhil* series continues with another meaningful message, as Phil the giant puppy teaches little readers that stress and anxiety are okay emotions to have, as long as they let someone know. This incredibly sweet story is filled with adorable illustrations. (Ages 3-12)

Dear Muslim Child

by Rahma Rodaah, Aya Ghanameh (Balzer & Bray)

Reviewer: Deb Greenberg

In this picture book from the author of *Dear Black Child*, Islam is revealed and uplifted for Muslim children. For readers who are not Muslim, it offers an understanding of the Islamic faith. The artwork shows the diversity that exists within Islam, adding meaning to the words on each page. (Ages 4-8)

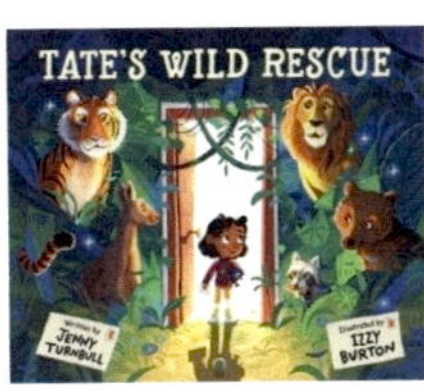

Tate's Wild Rescue

by Jenny Turnbull, Izzy Burton (Crown Books)

Reviewer: Kimberly Waters

Colorful animals and bright backgrounds bring Tate's world of rescue to life as she tries to save as many jungle animals as she can. Her letters are sincere and the responses from each animal are humorous as each one has an intriguing reason for not needing her help. Readers will smile at a little girl's sincerity as she finally finds the perfect one to save. The artwork is magnificent. Very well done! (Ages 4-8)

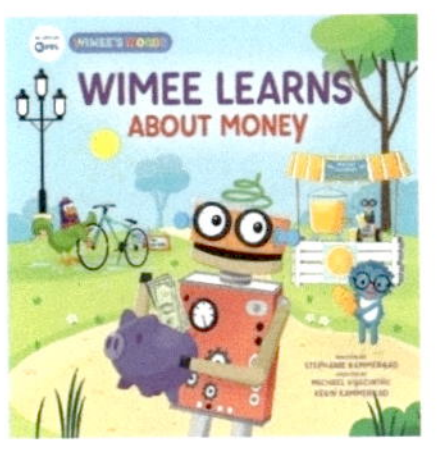

Wimee's Words: Wimee Learns About Money

by Stephanie Kammeraad, Kevin Kammeraad, Michael Hyacinthe (Zonderkidz)

Reviewer: Christine Irvin

Fans of the PBS series *Wimee's Words* will enjoy this latest book which features Wimee the robot. When Wimee receives some money from his grandmother, he's not sure what to do with it. Mr. Bill teaches Wimee and his friends about money and how it works. Kids who are not familiar with the series can still enjoy the bright, colorful illustrations and the informative text. (Ages 4-8)

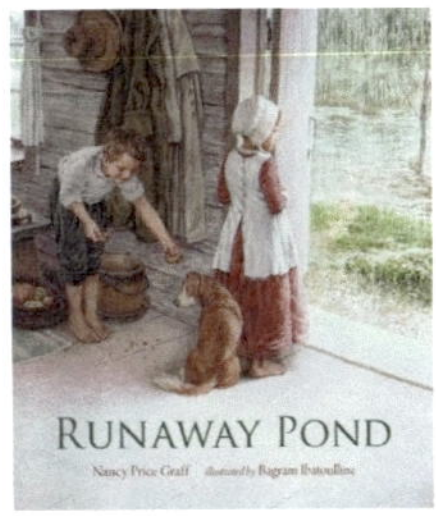

Runaway Pond

by Nancy Price Graff, Bagram Ibatoulline (Candlewick) Reviewer: Christine Irvin

Long Pond has been a source of joy and nourishment to a Vermont village for many years. But when a sudden late-summer storm causes the pond to swell and burst its banks, endangering everyone in its path, only one person is fast enough to warn the villagers downstream. It's an interesting tale with lots of great illustrations. (Ages 4-8)

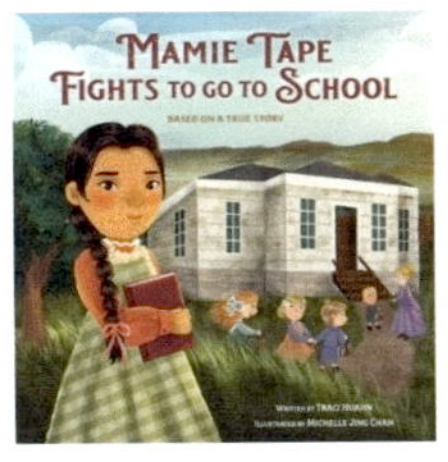

Mamie Tape Fights to Go to School

by Traci Huahn, Michelle Jing Chan (Crown Books) Reviewer: Christine Irvin

Mamie Tape is a Chinese American girl living in San Francisco in the 1880s. All she wants is to go to a real school. She faces many uphill battles in her fight for the right to attend public school. Author Traci Huahn tells Mamie's story, bringing history alive. She also includes several pages of additional information in the back of the book. This is a good story about the power of perseverance. (Ages 4-8)

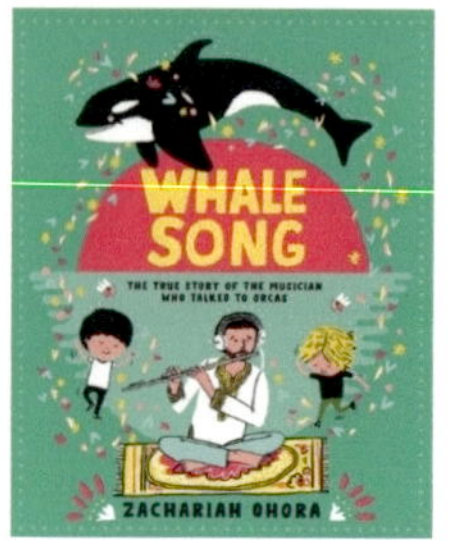

Whalesong: The True Story of the Musician Who Talked to Orcas

by Zachariah OHora (Tundra Books) Reviewer: Rachelle Stanger

This beautiful true story of musical communication with orcas is a reminder of the peace that orcas bring to our world. Musician Paul Horn and his children find a love for the orcas in the aquarium near their home, and find a special way to communicate with Paul's flute. With the help of Dr. Paul Spong, they reach a communication level unlike any other to help these whales in sickness and in health. (Ages 4-8)

Carla's Glasses

by Debbie Herman, Sheila Bailey (Flashlight Press) Reviewer: Kimberly Waters

It takes a clever mind to think up so many ways to make a pair of glasses! Carla is witty, silly, and caring and is an example of kindness we could all take a lesson from. Anybody who reads this will learn that a little bit of kindness goes a long, long way. In addition, the illustrator models her talent at creating a plethora of faces and expressions in a classroom of children who join in on the big surprise at the end! Well done! (Ages 5-8)

Swallows Swirl

by Christina Wilsdon, Jess Mason (Sleeping Bear Press)

Reviewer: Christine Irvin

A young girl keeps track of a flock of swallows on her farm as they progress through the year, building nests, raising their young, and catching bugs. When winter comes, she misses them as they fly south, but welcomes them when they return to the farm in the spring. Lyrical prose, lively illustrations, and repetitive text chronicle the life cycle of the swallows. Author Christian Wilsdon includes additional information about these birds in the back pages of the book. Kids can learn a lot about swallows all the while enjoying the story. (Ages 5-8)

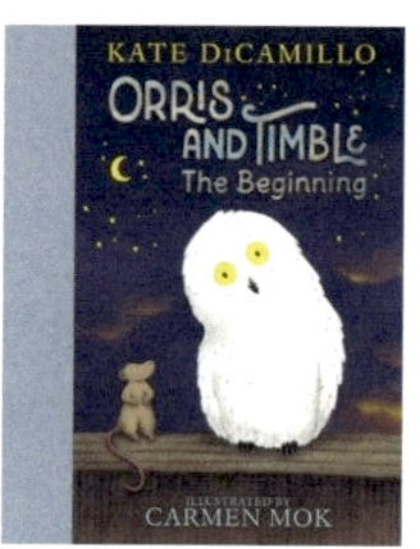

Orris and Timble: The Beginning

by Kate DiCamillo, Carmen Mok (Candlewick Press)

Reviewer: Deb Greenberg

The first book in this early-reader trilogy is about a rat and an owl, naturals foes but eventual friends. Friends? Is that possible? Owls eat rats, and Orris the rat is quite aware of that when Timble the owl gets caught in a trap in Orris's barn. Will Orris do the right thing? Another shining star from DiCamillo with full-color illustrations from Mok about the power of friendship and sharing stories that'll bring out the warm fuzzies in all of us. (Ages 5-8)

Frankie and Friends: The Big Protest

by Christine Platt, Alea Marley (Walker Books)

Reviewer: Christine Irvin

In the second book in this ongoing series, Frankie learns about journalism and protesting. Her mother is a journalist who covers breaking news stories. When Frankie's mom is sent to cover a protest, Frankie wants to report about protesting too. But she has a lot to learn first, like what a protest is and what people protest about. Frankie does research and conducts interviews, just like her mom does. This story provides a great introduction to the world of journalism. (Ages 5-8)

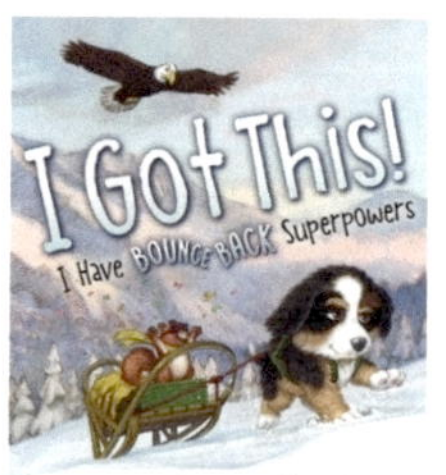

I Got This! I Have Bounce Back Superpowers

by Julia Cook, Michele Borba EdD, Dale Crawford (National Center for Youth Issues)

Reviewer:

Charlie has wanted to be a rescue dog since he was a puppy. But getting his certification as an official Rescue Dog requires a climb to the very top of the tallest mountain! With the help of his friends, and his six superpowers, will Charlie achieve his goal? Beautifully illustrated with real-world tools to help overcome fears and self-doubt and achieve your goals! YOU got this! (Ages 5-12)

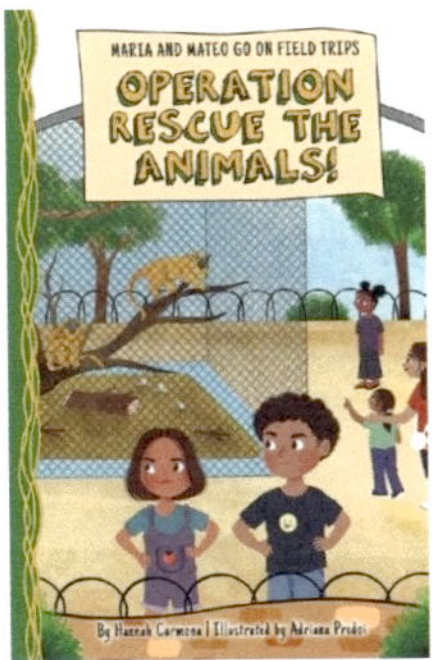

Maria and Mateo Go on Field Trips
by Hannah Carmona, Adriana Predoi (Jolly Fish Press)
Reviewer: Deb Greenberg

In this set of four books, cousins Maria and Mateo go on field trips with their class. The inquisitive pair learn as much about themselves as they do about their surroundings. In *Garden of Yuck!*, the pair are introduced to plants, flowers, and bugs. In *Fright at the Museum*, the kids are going on an overnight field trip to the Natural History Museum. *Operation Rescue the Animals* takes them to the zoo, where they have an overwhelming desire to let the animals roam free. In *Classical Catastrophe*, can the cousins keep an open mind when going on the orchestra field trip? The *Maria and Mateo* series is a simple yet fun and informative set of books. (Ages 6-8)

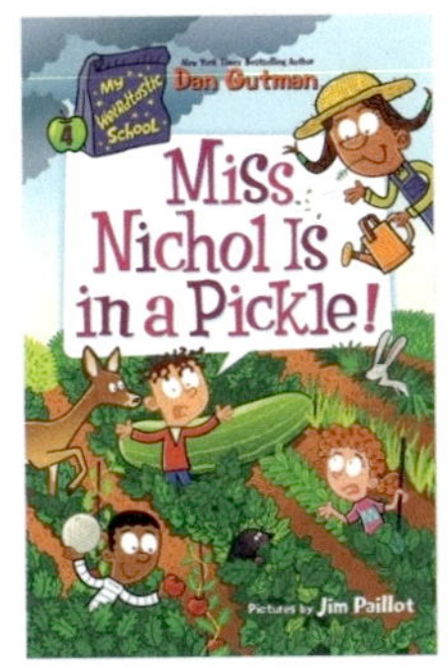

My Weirdtastic School: Miss Nichol Is in a Pickle!
by Dan Gutman, Jim Paillot (Harper Collins)
Reviewer: Deb Greenberg

Book 4 in the *My Weirdtastic School* series follows A.J. and his friends at Ella Mentry School, where Principal Stoker wants to start a vegetable garden. But the gang would rather plant junk food. Can gardening expert Miss Nichol keep things from spiraling out of control? Can they figure out who or what is eating their veggies? And what about that ginormous cucumber? Another super silly school story in the series kids will enjoy. (Ages 6-10)

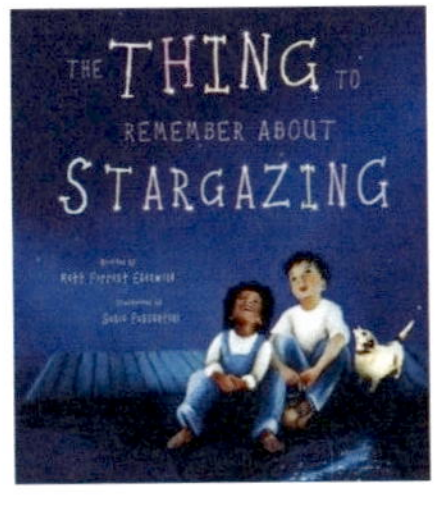

The Thing to Remember about Stargazing
by Matt Forrest Esenwine, Sonia Maria Luce Possentini (Tilbury House) Reviewer: Christine Irvin

When is the best time to stargaze? Should you do it by yourself or with someone else? What should you look for when you stargaze? All of these things are important, but there is one thing that is the most important. Can you guess what it is? Vivid illustrations with minimal yet vivid text are the perfect companions for this delightful book for any would-be astronomers or for those who just love to gaze at the stars. (Ages 7-10)

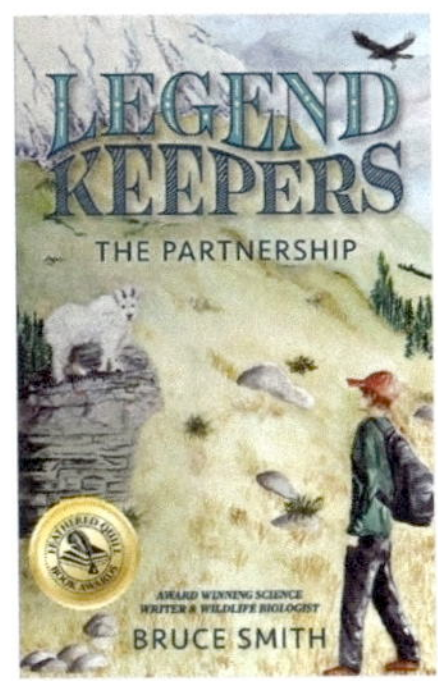

Legend Keepers: The Partnership
by Bruce Smith (Hidden Shelf Publishing)
Reviewer: Deb Greenberg

In the second book in the *Legend Keepers* series, Garson Strangewalker has trouble fitting in at his new school and in his new town. When a school science project leads him to the Shining Mountain Glacier in the wilderness, he meets Buddy, a young mountain goat. They're able to communicate and share an alarm over the Great Warming's threat to the glacier. Intriguing, adventurous, and filled with natural history details, interactions between nature and humans, and facts about climate change. (Ages 7-12)

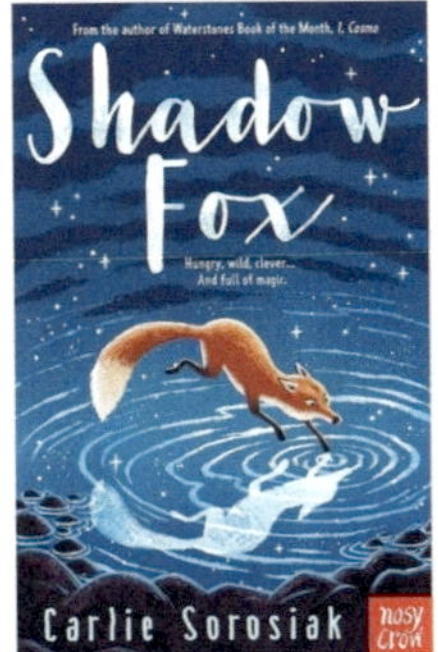

Shadow Fox
by Carlie Sorosiak (Walker Books)
Reviewer: Deb Greenberg

Can Shadow the fox rescue an island of people? The only human she likes is Nan because Nan feeds her fish every night. But when Nan disappears, things get quite fishy. A man from Whistlenorth Island comes ashore looking for Bee, who it turns out is Nan's granddaughter. Bee and Shadow develop a special bond as they embark on an adventure together to help Nan and rescue Whistlenorth Island from greedy, destructive Night Islanders. Narrated by Shadow, Sorosiak's story is an intriguing and adventurous one. (Ages 8-12)

Invisible Isabel
by Sally J. Pla, Tania de Regil (Quill Tree Books)
Reviewer: Kimberly Waters

It's a typical day in a typical elementary school where there is always a popular girl and her groupies, as well as a child who is introverted, shy, and invisible. The reader will recognize these kinds of children and maybe even compare them to someone they know. There are happy moments and sad moments, and moments when the reader will say, "Oh thank goodness someone cared." It is a well-written narrative and although it is fictional, it portrays reality in so many ways. Nicely done! (Ages 8-12)

The Great Animal Escape
by Linda Harkey (Story Monsters Press)
Reviewer: Raven Howell

What a fun surprise to end up chuckling through this delightful book! Linda Harkey deftly leads the reader into a world where several animals, quirky and comical in character, are escaping from a trip to Cowlick Ranch where they may become, well ... a meal. When troubles and disasters punctuate their newly hatched plan to get to the Cow Retirement Ranch, situations resolve with a touch of humor and whimsy. Illustrator Jeff Yesh's use of a pleasing palette of turquoise as a backdrop works superbly to depict the landscape intended. (Ages 8-12)

Chronicles of a Lizard Nobody
by Patrick Ness, Tim Miller (Walker Books)
Reviewer: Deb Greenberg

Monitor lizards Zeke, Daniel, and Alecia are hall monitors in Principal Wombat's school in the newest release from the best-selling author of *A Monster Calls*. Their duties are to impose order on the other animals in the school ... lions, seals, pandas, and an obnoxious school-bully pelican that has it out for the lizards. Together, with a blind red-tailed hawk, they attempt to protect their school of mismatched animals. Silly, hilarious, and filled with black-and-white illustrations. (Ages 9+)

Outspoken: Paul Robeson
by Carole Boston Weatherford, Eric Velasquez (Candlewick)
Reviewer: Larissa Juliano

Paul Robeson rose to prominence during the Harlem Renaissance, known for his extraordinary vocal, dramatic, and oratory skills. But he was a true Renaissance man: an accomplished athlete, a bright intellect, and a passionate supporter of humanitarian causes. This is a PERFECT discussion piece for students. The art design gorgeously captures Mr. Robeson's turbulent and unique life journey. (Ages 9-12)

To submit your book for review, email Cristy Bertini at cristy@storymonsters.com for submission guidelines.

GREEN TURTLE

(Chelonia mydas)

Animal Facts

Size:
3 to 4 feet

Weight:
240 to 420 pounds

Status:
Endangered

Veggies Only!

They live most of their lives underwater, and can stay below the surface up to five hours at a time before needing air!

Take a guess!
Turtle nests have an average of...

A. 50 eggs per nest
B. 15 eggs per nest
C. 525 eggs per nest
D. 115 eggs per nest

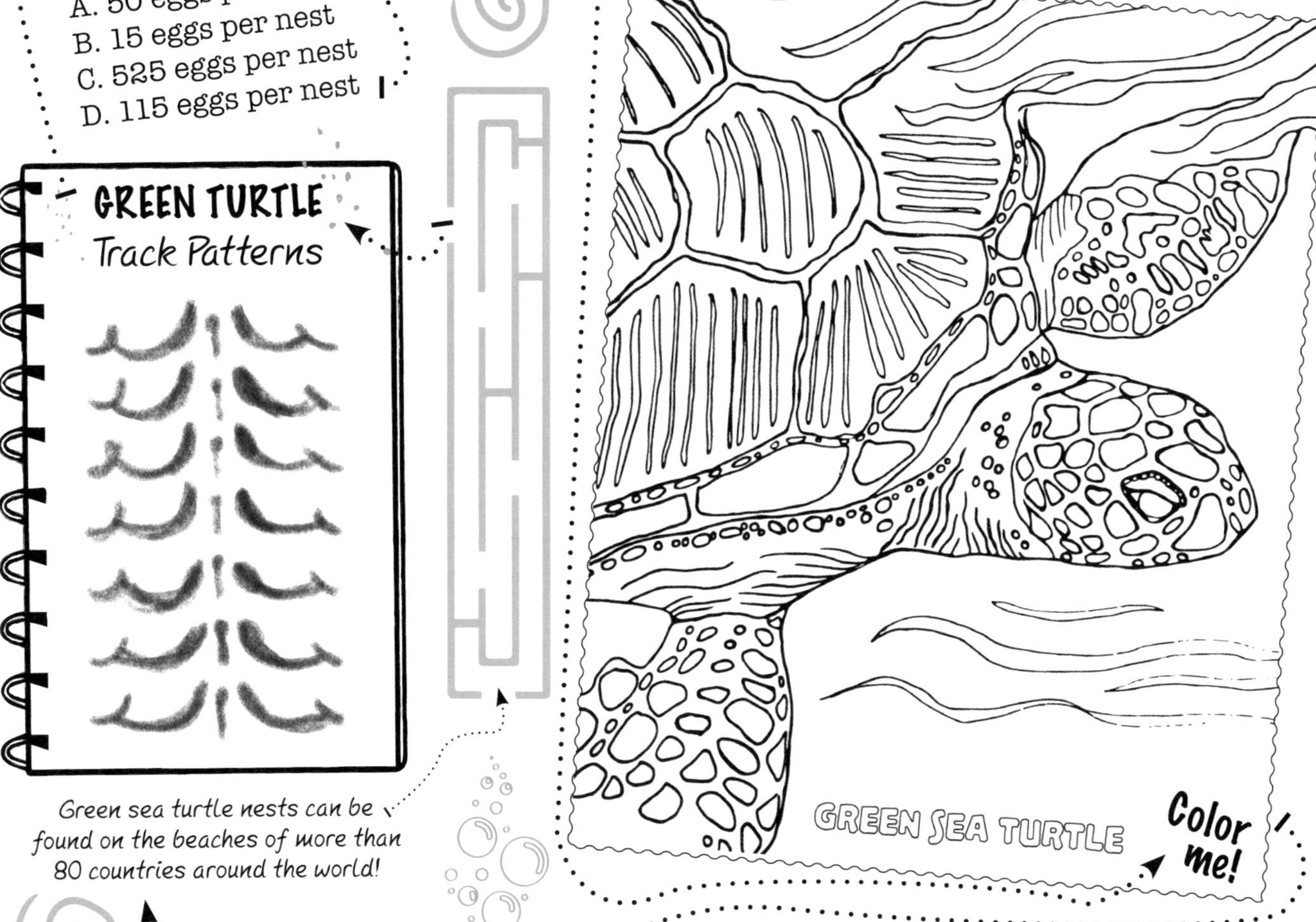

Green sea turtle nests can be found on the beaches of more than 80 countries around the world!

Answer is: D. 115 eggs per nest

Q&A WITH

DAN GEMEINHART

by Julianne Black DiBlasi

Do you ever wander into a memory of a childhood story? Something about your day, a smell, or a person you meet suddenly brings you back to an old favorite, and your feelings from that time spring at you like a retro pop-up book? Or did you ever wade through a bookstore with your own child and get the sensation you were in your own literary scrapbook, smiling at all the titles as you would a (great) class reunion?

The creatures, lessons, and characters from our favorite books create indelible grooves on the mind's greatest hits record, returning to the forefront at the oddest moments. Even as the seasons change and time passes, the memories from stories always stay with us—no matter how far we've traveled from when we first absorbed their wonder.

Once Upon a Friend is about exactly that. In the story, as soon as the reader opens Meego's book, the reader and main character become best friends. Together, they jump from the exciting adventures in Meego's stories to the fun times in their own life. Bravely exploring dark caves or facing big days like the first day of school, the reader and Meego go through everything together.

Whether you are feeling nostalgic, attempting to share the power of lifelong reading with your young ones, or simply in the mood for a great storytime book, *Once Upon a Friend* illuminates the magic of books and characters we never forget.

Q: Where did the idea come from for *Once Upon a Friend*, and what drove you to create your first picture book?

A: The idea for *Once Upon a Friend* came to me when I was visiting a middle school in Maine several years ago. The library had some stuffed animals of Elephant & Piggie on the shelf. It seemed like a funny decoration for a middle school, and when I asked the librarian about them, she said something along the lines of, "Well, middle school can be a scary place, and I think even these big kids like seeing old friends around." It made such an impression on me, and a line rose right into my mind: A friend you make in a book is a friend you never have to leave behind. The whole book kind of came out of that line.

Q: With empathy and kindness as major themes throughout the book, do you get many questions from readers about how to promote and explore those traits?

A: I'm not sure there's anything more important or necessary in the world than kindness and empathy. So many of the problems we face—as individuals, as a society, as a country—could be solved if we just put those two traits front and center. Anything that any one of us can do to push back against hatred, ignorance, and division is so important, now more than ever.

Q: What was it like seeing the illustrations for the first time? The bright and fun style of ShinYeon Moon's art is so tactile and dreamlike. Did you have a lot of say in how that part of the creative endeavor came to be?

A: I love the art in this book! It was absolutely goosebump-inducing incredible to see it for the first time. And I, thankfully, had almost nothing to do with it. ShinYeon did such a beautiful job bringing this story to life, and I definitely didn't want to get in

their way. I gave very small bits of occasional feedback, but honestly nothing very substantial. It is a remarkable feeling to see your own little words and story made real by such a talented artist!

Q: I love asking artists and writers to share their motivational tricks or routines that keep them on track. Is there anything you can share about how you personally handle writer's block or creative slumps?

A: It can be tough! I definitely get lost and mired down in the process sometimes. Sometimes I just keep at it, staring at the page and squeezing out words one at a time. Sometimes I walk away for a little reset and brain break. Sometimes I talk it out with my wife or kids. Sometimes I try working on something else to give my mind a chance to loosen up and get productive again. It can definitely be a struggle, though!

Q: What do you think is the most important element of a good story or the one question you remind yourself to revisit as you write?

A: Whenever I'm writing, I always think about the audience first and foremost. I know that my readers have a lot going on in their lives and a lot of things (and devices!) competing for

their attention, so I always want my stories to be entertaining and thoughtful, and to hopefully make them feel big things and think big thoughts.

Q: Your website mentions school visits! I'm sure you've had some wonderful experiences connecting with audiences of a variety of ages! Any moments stand out that you would like to share?

A: I spent 13 years as a public school librarian and I really miss it, so school visits are my favorite part of this job for sure! I've had the opportunity to visit schools all over the country, and even internationally. No one moment stands out, but it is always so fun to connect with readers and teachers and talk about books!

Q: I'm sure you are familiar with the analogy of the gold miner giving up just inches from a viable vein of ore. Your bio says you had worked 10 years before getting your first book published. What kept you going? Any advice you can share with our Story Monsters?

A: It was a long haul for sure! What kept me going was really just stubbornness, and a deep determination to get better. And, of course, a passionate love for books and stories! Even though I had a decade of, let's be honest, rejection and failure, I could see that I was getting better and improving. So my advice would definitely be to keep working, to focus not on your failures but on how you can get better, and to not get bitter or disillusioned; remember why you started in the first place, and keep that in mind as you work on getting better!

Q: What's next for you and how can we follow your adventures?

A: Thanks for asking! I've got a lot of fun stuff on the horizon. I've got another middle grade novel and picture book coming out next year, both of which I'm super excited about, and then a third picture book coming out in 2026. I feel so lucky to be doing what I'm doing. You can follow me on Twitter and Instagram at @dangemeinhart. Thanks for your questions!

For more information about Dan Gemeinhart and his work, visit dangemeinhart.com.

Julianne Black DiBlasi • Mom, wielder of pixel, paint, and pen. krakenSky.com

CONSTANCE LOMBARDO AND MICAH PLAYER

Have Created a (Good) Monster

by Raven Howell

When picture book and middle-grade author/illustrator Constance Lombardo describes Itty Bitty Betty Blob from her new book as "a blob who loves swaying more than stomping, who chooses rainbows over ruination, and who tries to be bad, like a good little monster, but simply cannot," I'm hooked.

Constance's enthusiasm for her newly written character is contagious. "Betty is exactly the kind of free-spirited visionary I seek out in my friends," she divulges. "We would definitely dance among the dandelions together. Maybe even bake a cake with pink frosting!"

In the book, *Itty Bitty Betty Blob*, Betty is not your typical monster. She practices growling and scowling for picture day at school but ultimately doesn't enjoy scaring other people. It's an endearing journey of discovering and embracing our differences, and Betty ends up inspiring those around her. The mood of the plot and tone of the artwork morph from the drearier black and whites of emotional struggles and insecurities to the colorful enjoyment of making new friends and feeling accepted.

"Betty is truly her own blob, with a sunny disposition and unique way of moving through the world ... literally! I hope she helps kids see that being yourself, even when the world has different expectations, is a righteous and courageous act."

Constance notes, "My son is transgender, and while this connection did not occur to me until the book was almost done, I believe Betty counters the current push from certain sectors for a return to 1950s-style gender roles and rigid thinking in general."

The book sparkles with a fun, uplifting perspective. "What I hope is fresh is the humor, this particular world of monsters so beautifully created by artist Micah Player, and the total acceptance of Betty by her schoolmates and mother. One of my favorite pages has Betty and Mom dancing to a record on an old-fashioned gramophone ... so joyful. I'm happy we've moved

away from the concept of 'tolerance.' I feel differences should be celebrated! That's what *Itty Bitty Betty Blob* does—through the story and hugely through Micah's amazing artwork. It's a celebration! Let's get this party started!"

Constance found herself writing much of the story from the "wonderful abundance of groovy cafes with cranberry scones and oat milk matcha lattes" in her hometown in Western NC. Her editor encouraged revisions and coaxed Constance to go deeper. "My original title was *Picture Day at Monster School*, but *Itty Bitty Betty Blob* was always the star of the story. My wonderful editor, Jill Davis, suggested Betty's name as the title, and she was right! It's so fun to say."

"I wrote *Picture Day at Monster School* totally focused on that particular day and sort of fell in love with it, which is never a good idea! Revisions always involve painful moments, 'killing your darlings,' and sometimes numerous complete rewrites. I think the page from the book with monsters in front of the camera—"Fleas! Click! Bees! Click! Scabby Knees!"—may be the only original lines that made it into the final book. But it all happened exactly as it should. And I am incredibly proud of this book," she concludes.

Itty Bitty Betty Blob's illustrator, Micah Player, has illustrated several books including, *Paletero Man*, *Chloe*, *Instead*, and *Vote for our Future*. But years before book illustration, Micah designed characters and graphics for the apparel industry.

He explains, "My degree is in graphic design. I loved the whole discipline of type, layout, and setting the tone for something, whether that was a company or ad campaign or product. So even though I loved picture books and was always scribbling ideas for characters and stories, the professional destination, especially what we talked about in school, seemed to be an ad agency or design studio."

'When it was time to line up an internship for the summer of my Junior year, I reached out to a friend who was working at Paul Frank Industries," he recalls. "I was so lucky to get

that opportunity. When I was there, I had a ton of freedom to experiment and collaborate with both the veteran artists and designers who had been there from the beginning and other new kids who were putting things together in all these unexpected ways. It was awesome and challenging and just a unicorn first job out of school."

"Our licensing director was always looking for new partners, and eventually we got the opportunity to work with Chronicle Books to do a series of picture books, games, and stationery featuring *Julius the Monkey* and his friends."

"It was in the process of illustrating a book for that series that I got to know my first editor, then at Chronicle Books. I showed her some other things I had been sketching and she loved them and told me if I was ever interested in doing something based on my own stuff to give her a call. About a year later, that's what I did, and it changed my life."

Asked to describe his artwork succinctly, Micah says, "Emotionally expressive characters rendered as simply as I can manage.

"Designing Betty and her world was so much fun. It is rare to create such a from-scratch environment where there are no iconic monsters, just a world of things. I love *The Adams Family* and *Where the Wild Things Are*, monsters that are their own gothic ecosystem rather than riffing on fairy tales or classic movies.

"With Betty, I wanted to have a predominantly dreary/dark palette for the world she lived in, but I wanted it to be rich for the reader. So rather than a straight black, I rendered it in a super dark brown, almost black, with a natural tone for the whites. Betty's warm pink was intended to be this glow that casts a little color wherever she goes and is easy to spot for young eyes. When she meets the Puff characters, they, like her, also cast a little bit of color, which for them is a whole rainbow."

In the story, Betty hopes her school picture will find a place on the family portrait wall. And when Betty's mom proclaims, "It's so perfectly you," love prevails. Micah says, "Betty's journey is about allowing herself to fully connect with the people around her and the students at school, but also in a way that is meaningful to me, her parent. Betty's mom is a good mom!"

Constance is grateful to have collaborated with Micah. "I'm someone who plays well with others, and working on a picture book is absolutely a collaborative process," she says. "I can let go of my ego and appreciate what my editor, illustrator, and art director bring. It's an exciting journey! Also, I have the ability to be flexible."

Constance is the author/illustrator of the popular *Mr. Puffball* series. "I was surprised by how much the *Mr. Puffball* books appeal to kids who think of themselves as 'not into reading.' I love that *Mr. Puffball* has gotten some kids into the joy of books! And bonus that he's beloved by kids who share my quirky sense of humor and love of puns!"

In addition, she wrote and illustrated the adorably whimsical *Everybody Says Meow* (HarperCollins) and wrote *Tiny Spoon Vs Little Fork* (Hippo Park). "I'm all about drawing and ink. Watercolor is a difficult beast and I wildly admire artists who use it well! I rely on a simple wash. I try to let the simple beauty of the color shine through."

She considers herself an extrovert, saying, "Being out among friends, maybe at a local Trivia Night or Game Night (Pictionary, please!), or jumping into a cool waterfall pool on a hot day make me happy. Hanging out with my son rewatching *Lord of the Rings*, probably eating nachos."

When Micah's not illustrating, he's often writing songs or playing music and loves traveling to new places with his kids and Steph, his wife of 25 years. He's excited about an upcoming picture book he wrote and illustrated, titled *This is a Moment*, releasing next year.

Constance is currently working "on something to self-publish as a zine, for adults, with art in black and white. I'd like to stretch my wings with something completely different and personal. And I'm thrilled to say there will be a second *Betty* book. I'm super excited, especially to be working again with Micah!

"The love for Betty has been amazing!" she exclaims. "I recently did an event at Books are Magic in Brooklyn. When I walked in and introduced myself to one of the lovely booksellers, her eyes lit up, and she said, 'We love Betty SO much!' That is everything to me."

Micah echoes the love and inspiration *Itty Bitty Betty Blob* is providing. "For kids, the message is that bringing your whole self to everything you do is worthwhile and wonderful. There is a place for exactly who you are in your family and in the world," he says. "For parents, the message is that nothing in life is more precious than their relationship with the little people they have the privilege to protect, guide, and get to know. Whatever you might imagine or assume about who your kids might be, who they actually are is better."

But the final words come straight from *Itty Bitty Betty Blob's* Betty: "You are perfect just as you are!"

For more information about Constance Lombardo and Micah Player and their work, visit constancelombardo.com and micahplayer.com. ●

Raven Howell is an award-winning children's author and poet. ravenhowell.com

URBAN BIRD WATCHING: RAPTORS

by Conrad J. Storad

We all know the iconic images:

A bald eagle soars through a cobalt blue sky, white-capped mountain peaks in the background.

Wings spread and talons extended, a red-tailed hawk dives on unsuspecting prey.

Large eyes unblinking, a great horned owl watches from the trees.

Raptors are fascinating. They are meat-eating birds that share several key characteristics. All raptors have keen eyesight. They have eight razor-sharp talons. And all have sharp, hooked beaks used for tearing and shredding flesh.

These big birds of prey have existed in some form on Earth for almost 75 million years. According to information posted by the Raptor Center at the University of Minnesota, there are 482 species of raptor on Earth today.

But it was not that long ago that many raptor species were in deep danger right here in the United States. During the early 1960s, scientists knew that many raptor populations were in decline. The peregrine falcon, osprey, and our national bird, the bald eagle, were all headed for extinction.

The culprit was identified later in the decade. It was the pesticide dichloro-diphenyl-trichloroethane, commonly known as DDT.

DDT was a superb insect killer. It was one of the first synthetic pesticides used during World War II. DDT wiped out mosquitoes that spread malaria, typhus, and other diseases among soldiers and civilian populations.

The damage it caused raptors and other animals was discovered later. Widely used during the 1950s and 1960s, the powerful poison worked its way up through the food chain. DDT caused egg-shell thinning in many bird species. Eggs would crack before a chick could hatch. The poison led to overall reproductive failure among eagles, falcons, ospreys, and other birds of prey. They appeared doomed.

The Osprey's razor sharp talons are designed for catching fish.

In 1970, President Richard Nixon and Congress approved the establishment of the Environmental Protection Agency to protect the environment and human health. DDT was totally banned in 1972. Raptors also benefited from other federal laws, including the Endangered Species Act in 1973.

Today, eagles and other raptors symbolize the best of what ecological-minded science and environmental consciousness can accomplish. But you don't have to go to the mountains or national parks to see them. Eagles, hawks, falcons, ospreys, and other raptors have adapted to life in big cities, small towns, and right in our own backyards.

It's almost impossible for a raptor to "sneak" into your backyard. Jays or cardinals will screech shrill warnings. Squirrels will scatter and flatten themselves against tree trunks. The yard will go silent.

When that happens, stop, look, and listen. Scan the rooftops and branches high in the trees. Then wait. You might be in for a show.

The neighbors might need a bigger birdbath.

Raptor fun facts:

- According to the Raptor Center at the University of Minnesota, there are 304 diurnal (day-active) species of raptors. There are 178 nocturnal species.
- What if you had eagle vision? You could spot an ant crawling on the sidewalk while standing on the roof of a 10-story building.
- Eagles can fly almost 100 miles per hour and soar as high as 15,000 feet.
- Ospreys have a reversible outer toe. This allows them to grab and hold prey with two talon-tipped toes in front and two behind. Barbed pads on the soles of the bird's feet allow them to grip slippery fish. When flying with prey, the big hawk usually bites off the head first to keep a still-living fish from snapping at it while in flight.
- Hawks live for an average of 12 years in the wild. But under the right conditions, a Red-tailed hawk can live for as long as 30 years.

A cool drink on a sweltering hot July day for this Red-tailed Hawk.

Ahhhhhhh. Now that feels nice on a stinking hot summer afternoon.

Learn more about urban raptors:

Books/Websites:

- *The Urban Birder*
  —by David Lindo and Stephen Moss
- *Urban Tales: A Birdwatching Diary*
  —by Andreas Stockmannv
- Cornell University Laboratory of Ornithology
  https://merlin.allaboutbirds.org
- Birda birdwatching app
  https://birda.org
- Roost – The Urban Birder
  https://theurbanbirder.com
- The Raptor Center at The University of Minnesota
  https://raptor.umn.edu/
- HawkWatch International
  https://hawkwatch.org

A Cooper's hawk outside the back window.

Ospreys build large, loose nests out of sticks and twigs.

Everyone hide! The Cooper's hawk is looking for lunch.

Conrad J. Storad is the national award-winning author or editor of more than 50 science and nature books for children and young adults. His first book in a new series, *Night Watchers: Nocturnal Creatures of North America*, is out now.
conradjstorad.com

Betty has a message just for you! Can you work out what it is?

A	B	C	D	E	F	G	H	I	J	K	L	M
1	2	3	4	5	6	7	8	9	10	11	12	13
N	O	P	Q	R	S	T	U	V	W	X	Y	Z
14	15	16	17	18	19	20	21	22	23	24	25	26

__   __ __   __ __ __ __ __ __ __ __
9   1 13   7 18 1 20 5 6 21 12

__ __ __   __ __ __   __ __ __ !
25 15 21   1 18 5   25 15 21

My Grandma and the Piano

by Olivia Amiri, age 16

I must've been around seven or eight, because the memory is soft like gauze and waterlogged with emotion. Tired, I walked the hallway from my room toward the sound of loud adults in the living room. In my nightgown I stood in the foyer, watching the group of adults who had not yet registered my presence. My grandmother was at the piano, sitting with her torso turned away from the keys.

The piano wasn't for music making, and I couldn't play anything even resembling a song. I could play a storm and thunder until my fists hurt, or I could tap my nails on the highest keys at random. The piano was like a disrespected horse. I would put my juice cups on its back, and stickers on its imitation ivory. Laying on my stomach on its bench, I moved my arms like I was swimming. When I had friends over, we leaned our backs against its wooden legs and played with marbles until we lost them.

Hovering near the piano room, I was tempted then to run and hit upon its keys; I was tempted to start a storm that would catch the adults' attention so that they would applaud me—or run for cover. But before I could start, my grandma started to play, and the conversation stopped to listen. I know it was beautiful, but I can't remember what she played. All I can remember is how enraptured everyone was, barely blinking and silent as they could be.

When I would command my mom to watch me cartwheel or begged my dad to stop and watch me play a game on his phone, they always watched for a moment, and then quickly moved on. But I think if my grandmother had continued to play for hours, they wouldn't have moved from their seats. The old woman was focused, like she looked when she braided my hair or spatchcocked a chicken. She handled the keys like she was mastering them; for a moment I saw her strength. Just as when she would section my hair so tight that the braid would stay for days, or when she cut away the bird's cartilage and ran a sharp knife cutting its back in two. I wanted her precision. I wanted her strength.

Standing in the foyer, hot jealousy ran through me like I had been showered with it. It wasn't fair—I couldn't stop that feeling, but it wasn't far from love; it was an admiration so strong that it became something desperate. The next morning, I ran to the piano bench. I tried to claim the keys and make them sing like she had, but the frustrated noise was all my hands could create. I stopped playing the violin; every day I would sit straight-backed on the bench and try again to play something that would make my parents stop and listen.

Ten years later, I am a "better" player than my grandmother. But I don't remember the point anymore; my hands make people stop and listen, but usually when my audience is captivated, it is made up of strangers. My family has heard me play so much that it has become background noise, like the dishwasher running or the fax machine. Her playing was special because it was rare, like seeing a snowflake in spring or spotting a hawk flying overhead on the highway. •

Sixteen-year-old Olivia Amiri is a little girl with big advice! Sharing insights and observations on the world around us, her message is clear: kids are still the best teachers to remind grown-ups of the simple joys in life. livonlife.com

GET READY FOR SOME TAIL-WAGGING ADVENTURES!
SOLITARY TOES AND BROWN-HEADED COWBIRDS
THE REMARKABLE STORY OF WILLIE THE CROW
LINDA HARKEY
Hickory Doc's Tales
DOC, WILLIE, AND THE PACK: SECRETS, GIFTS, FAMILY
DOC'S DOG
written by Linda Harkey illustrated by Mike Minick
Chatty the Hen Pheasant
Travels With The Pack
NEW!
Award-winning books for elementary-age children
www.harkeybooks.com
Available at archwaypublishing.com and amazon.com
@harkeybooks

Made in the USA
Columbia, SC
25 September 2024